"In the noisy, fast-paced culture we
that has been forgotten: the art of ap
of being still. In *Finding Quiet*, Jamie Grace gives us more clarity on the importance of understanding that slowing down can be the place that we hear God's voice the clearest. My encouragement to you is to take to heart and put into practice what Jamie Grace says so eloquently in this book."

—Anthony Evans, artist, author, and worship leader

"*Finding Quiet* is such powerful insight into the heart of what makes Jamie one of my favorite humans. Her balance of the noise and the quiet have inspired me to pursue the same balance in my career and my everyday life."

— Melinda Doolittle, recording artist, author,
Melinda Doolittle Entertainment

"Jamie Grace is brutally, deeply, dangerously honest about herself. (And that's why this book is going to be a blessing to so many who will think, *Her too? I thought I was the only one.*) There's something freeing about deep introspection coupled with real, life-giving, hard-won wisdom. And that's what Jamie Grace is giving us."

—Brant Hansen, radio host and author of *The Truth About Us*, *Unoffendable*, and *Blessed Are the Misfits*

"Jamie Grace brings all of herself to this book, *Finding Quiet*. Her stories are honest and raw. Her voice is tender and loving, and the tone of this book is nothing but encouraging. As a woman who has done lots of hard work to find her quiet, Jamie Grace will help you find yours as well! If you are feeling like this world is roaring with noises, like I often do, pick this book up and begin to devour her words. She's the friend you always wanted, inviting you into her experiences and sharing what truths she has found from Scripture to help you on your journey in life. Thank you, Jamie Grace, for these words!"

—Jamie Ivey, bestselling author and host of
The Happy Hour with Jamie Ivey podcast

"For someone who is known for making music, sharing a message of *Finding Quiet* is a strong and beautiful testament to Jamie Grace's wisdom and growth as an artist, woman, and believer. Jamie Grace has a way of sharing hope for others in search of peace, in a relatable (and oftentimes hilarious) way. It is conversational and contemplative, heartwarming and thought-provoking. In *Finding Quiet*, you will feel heard and seen."

—Morgan Harper Nichols, artist and poet

"I've toured with Jamie and have watched her pour her soul out so that others could experience God's grace, love, and power. In her new book, she's at it again! Marinate in each chapter and you'll gain wisdom, encouragement, and inspiration."

—Tony Nolan, evangelist, mentor, and pastor

Finding Quiet

Finding Quiet

MY JOURNEY TO PEACE IN AN ANXIOUS WORLD

JAMIE GRACE

BETHANYHOUSE
a division of Baker Publishing Group
Minneapolis, Minnesota

Published by Bethany House Publishers
11400 Hampshire Avenue South
Bloomington, Minnesota 55438
www.bethanyhouse.com

Bethany House Publishers is a division of
Baker Publishing Group, Grand Rapids, Michigan

Printed in the United States of America

ISBN 978-0-7642-3607-5 (cloth)
ISBN 978-0-7642-3823-9 (trade paper)

This book recounts events in the life of Jamie Grace according to the author's recollection and information from the author's perspective. While all stories are true, some dialogue and identifying details have been changed to protect the privacy of the people involved.

Cover design by Dan Pitts
Cover photo by Cat Harper Photography

Author is represented by Good Eye Management.

20   21   22   23   24   25   26   7   6   5   4   3   2   1

To the over-thinkers and hopeful believers,
and to the anxious hearts that are graciously beating,
we have our fears, insecurities, doubts, and setbacks,
yet seldom give ourselves credit for how far we've come.

So let's silence the noise that says we cannot achieve,
let's embrace the silence whose joy is noisy.
To the children, men, and women who are anything like me,
let's remember we are fighters, and there is a grace
that covers every one of our needs.

CONTENTS

PROLOGUE

JAMIE GRACE! JAMIE GRACE! JAMIE GRACE!

The crowd chanted as I stood offstage in a unicorn onesie.

I had just turned twenty-five and was celebrating by releasing the song "Party Like a Princess" and doing a concert a day later in Minnesota, one of my favorite places to perform.

(A little backstory on the onesie: I started my career by making YouTube videos, so a lot of people who know my music have also watched a lot of the comedic and lifestyle videos I share on my channel. One thing that has weaved its way into these videos is my love for wearing onesies—and unicorn onesies in particular.)

I had decided that at the end of the show, we would black out the lights and I would run backstage, change into a onesie, and return to perform an encore of "Party Like a Princess."

While I knew that a lot of people had bought and streamed the song online, I wasn't prepared for what happened next.

As I headed back to the stage after changing, I heard the chants.

JAMIE GRACE! JAMIE GRACE! JAMIE GRACE!

I was overwhelmed and excited but also a bit nervous. While the song had reached number one on iTunes the day it was released—just one day before the concert—I was slightly worried that doing an encore with a song less than twenty-four hours old might have been an odd choice.

But the second the song started, with its intense bass line and drums, the crowd went wild.

They know it! I thought.

I walked onto the stage and began singing and, to my surprise, almost everyone in the room sang my words back to me. I kept looking to the side of the stage where Morgan, my sister and best friend, stood, as if to ask, *Are you seeing this? Are you hearing this?*

This was the first song I had released since leaving a record label and becoming an independent artist. The concert was booked and promoted through my own management and not by a major booking company. I was blown away to see how many people believed in me. I could barely process how much they were supporting me.

I had a message I wanted to share, songs I was passionate about, and I was so grateful that every little dream in my heart was coming true.

Halfway through the song, I made a spontaneous decision to talk over the music, inviting every girl in the crowd wearing a onesie to come onstage and dance with me. The girls rushed the stage, and the energy in the crowd carried itself onto the platform as we jumped, sang, and screamed. It was one of the most memorable moments of my entire life.

My Career Is Far from Quiet

Even when I'm in the studio and it needs to be quiet so I can get a clear recording, it's *still* loud. Before recording, I check the room to make sure I won't be faced with any unexpected noise—including the low hums and rumbles of my laptop (it's really old and I'm really frugal) as it tries to load software, or the sudden starts and stops of the air conditioner desperately fighting against the Southern California heat. Any sound, big or small, must be silenced so that the quality of the recording is not compromised. Yet once I actually find the quiet I've been looking for, I press Record, and the quiet dissipates as I start singing or playing guitar.

It's *never* truly quiet. Whether I'm in the studio, attending an event or a meeting, performing, or doing an interview, it's rare that I find myself embracing quiet, and for more than ten years this has been my reality.

When I was nineteen years old, I was nominated for a Grammy for a song I had written while sitting on the floor of my dorm room. I was the youngest nominee that year, and I went home as the Dove Awards New Artist of the Year, with three other nominations. I would later see myself on 7UP cans around the country, as the winner of a fan-voted award through K-Love radio.

My next four radio singles would go on to be number ones; my songs would be on rotation at major retail stores, in commercials for Belk and Dell, and even on reality shows on VH1 and MTV. I would get phone calls and emails from NFL players and politicians from various parties whose children were big fans of my music, offering tickets to major games and events in exchange for my creating a video greeting to someone for Christmas or a birthday. There was even a moment when my song was played on ESPN *accidentally* because one of the announcers had it as a ringtone and forgot to silence his phone while broadcasting.

I found myself performing on *The View*, and ended up taking home a pair of Whoopi Goldberg's shoes that she took off and handed to me. And I sang a duet with my *favorite* artist, Reba McEntire, at her request.

While I was humbled and excited by all the success, it often seemed increasingly difficult to find quiet.

For most of my years in the public eye, I was single. I made videos and songs about being content in my singlehood while at the same time praying that I would someday get married. I approached the topic with humor and a little bit of attitude—gracefully, of course—and began to receive emails from girls, teens, and women in their twenties and thirties thanking me for being vulnerable and open about my story.

Kids all around the world were dancing to my music with their friends and classmates, and sometimes moms would tell me that I helped keep their children on a good path. College students would tell me that my songs were a part of their hope and support system as they grew up and as things in their lives begin to change.

While I was humbled and excited by all the success, it often seemed increasingly difficult to find quiet.

As I was growing up and leaning into my passion for music and the gift God had given me, some of my most joyful and peaceful times were late at night when it was just me and my piano or guitar. At night I tried to keep the recording to a minimum; it was my assurance that I would be honest and sincere, and use my songs as a time to pray instead of work—the exception being when I felt led to document something for a later time.

I would sing about things I was thankful for and things I didn't understand. I would sing worship songs from church and make some up on the spot. I would write songs full of joy as well as lyrics that were sometimes too painful to sing.

Then, I listen.

I enjoy sitting in the space where everything is laid at God's feet and the expectation is to hear what He has to say. There was never the presumption that it would be a major announcement from heaven with glowing lights and a play-by-play of upcoming miracles, but I *did* find peace in the quiet and hope in those moments with the Lord.

But somehow, as my career grew and changed, I felt the need to change too. There was no more time for late nights of spontaneous writing and listening, and I succumbed to the pressure that any time I made music, it should be made into a moment. The joy in writing to worship was gone, and my number-one priority became writing for work.

I had always written songs in hopes of connecting with my feelings or with the feelings of the listener, but as the pressure mounted, it seemed like feelings became a currency. Every career high reinforced that it wasn't about how I could use the pain, joy, and beauty of life to find quiet moments to listen, be challenged, and grow. Instead, the goal was to use the noise to fuel even more and to avoid simplicity at whatever cost.

But that's not who I was. It's not who I am. And in the moments that may have seemed that I was at my highest, I was often drowning in the deep end, searching for the voice that always spoke. I simply had to listen.

Growing Up, Quiet Was Easier to Find

One of my earliest memories of growing up in the '90s is when I fell in love with Jesus. I was only seven years old, and it wasn't a romanticized concept of Jesus being my boyfriend or superhero. It was a quiet moment with my dad as he led me through a prayer that I wanted to pray, accepting Jesus to be a part of my life forever.

Thinking back to that day, I don't remember what room we were in. I don't know the exact date it happened, and I certainly have no recollection of what I was wearing or what I had for dinner later that night. But I specifically remember the sounds, as I know for a fact that there weren't many.

When I gave my life over to God and decided to follow Christ, I was overwhelmed with a peace and resolve that could only be explained as something spiritual even though it translated into the physical. I wasn't persuaded or pushed into making a decision, I simply knew it was what I wanted, and my dad helped me take the next step.

God doesn't move any more or less in rooms because of their volume or lack thereof. Yet for me, someone whose mind is constantly competing in a relay race of passing the baton, trigger after trigger, my heart stood still when God met me in the quiet. Because that was a place I craved more than anything.

I was surrounded by a lot of sounds in my childhood: We lived near an old train track that had the most inconsistent midnight hours; there were *many* outdoor dogs in our neighborhood, including mine; and I'm a preacher's kid, so our days and evenings in church were full of music, conversation, and sermons that were as deep as they were loud.

But I still managed to find quiet.

My mom—a homeschooler and pastor with a knack for interior design that made our house feel and look like it belonged in a magazine—loves quiet. And that's a little ironic because she and I both are outgoing and talkative, and if we can get the whole room laughing, it's a good day. But she would always recharge in silence.

When my mom, my sister, and I would drive to one of our homeschool groups, or when the whole family was driving to church, she would often turn off the radio and encourage us to just listen. Sometimes we would end up having deep conversations about culture, and other times we would end up cracking jokes and telling funny stories. But many times we would just sit in the quiet.

That was difficult for me. I would rather talk and tell jokes. But I knew that there would always be a safe place for me to find quiet if and when I needed it.

Morgan and my dad are naturally quiet.

As many similarities as I have with my mom, they have their own as well. My dad is an electrician by trade and is also a pastor. There's no way he could wire houses and troubleshoot *any* electrical issue if he didn't have the incredible ability to focus in the quiet. And my sister is very much like him. She's well-known as a poet and artist, and so much of her work takes intentional focus and concentration. They are both disciplined in a way that, to me, is a learned skill.

I remember when my dad took Morgan and me camping for the first time.

We were around nine and seven years old.

We drove out to the woods, where my dad set up the tent to get ready for our daddy-daughters weekend. I don't remember everything about the trip, but I do remember that both Morgan and my dad were acting as though it was completely normal to put a tent in the woods. I remember them working in silence to get everything ready, and my disbelief grew as I slowly processed that I would be expected to sleep there.

I started asking questions about where we would sleep (just to make sure), what and how we would eat, and where we would go to the bathroom—to which my dad replied by just showing me a bucket.

Looking back, I can see that they were pursuing an evening of both quiet and adventure, of peace and freedom. But I was far from interested in pursuing it myself. So I asked my dad if he would take me home. And he did.

That was the last time I went camping.

While I am still positive that camping is not for me, I'm grateful to have the kind of dad who pushed me to try something out of my comfort zone and the kind of sister who was ready to try something new too. And I'm grateful to have the kind of mom who went, and still goes, against the mold, whether it's in regard to design or car rides, always challenging the status quo.

That was the essence of my childhood. It was peculiar and out of the ordinary—and everything I could have ever wanted. My parents were, and still are, madly in love with each other, graciously committed to us girls, and passionate about being missionary and founding pastors of our intimate local church.

Our home was full of learning, music, and really, really good food. We were not perfect. We seldom had money for extra-curricular actives, and sometimes not even for rent. But we were honest. We were joyful. We were trustworthy and full of love. And years later, we still have a connection and a bond that's unmatchable.

We were loud—even on the days when my sister and I were reading, our mom was working on an art project, and our dad was reconfiguring one of our electronics. Our love and joy reached a decibel level that resonated throughout our home and our lives, whether we were making sounds or not.

So when it came to finding quiet, that was easy. Peace seemed to go hand in hand with any moment that we faced.

Yes, life was challenging. We had disagreements, like any other family, and as a pastor's family, we were seldom in our home without others who needed our support. But somehow, in the midst of the noise, we would always find quiet.

We didn't have a lot of money for bookstores, but we loved books, so our mom took us on trips to the library. We fell in love with the smell of books and the soft sound of the pages turning.

We stayed late after church most Sundays, and we got there early, before the sound system was even turned on. We could hear the soft creaking of the wood floor as we walked up and down the aisle, listening to our dad practice his sermon.

Somehow, in the craziness and busyness of childhood, we always found quiet.

This Book Is All about Finding Quiet

But it is *not* about learning to tune out every sound. God can speak to us even in the midst of noise. He can speak to us even while our minds and our ears are being filled with other sounds. God *does* speak to us in the middle of the noise and the sounds and even the mundane and the simple. God is always moving, always speaking, and it's up to *us* to find quiet.

Somehow, in the craziness and busyness of childhood, we always found quiet.

Life is full of noise, sound, and occasional reckless volume that we wish we could shut out. And sometimes we can. Sometimes we can step away, break away, move away from the commotion that causes us to feel like we're drowning in turmoil.

But other times, we can't silence the noise.

We can simply hope to find quiet while the sound plays on.

As I've gotten older, there have been many unexpected moments in my life. From health challenges to friendships falling apart to pursuing living out my dream career, I have faced my fair share of both highs and lows. They have all had the potential to become so overwhelming that I would forget how to step back, take a deep breath, and embrace quiet—and sometimes I have.

In this book, I share the day-to-day of finding quiet. Together, we'll journey through things such as learning to let go, comparison, friendships, relationships, purpose, and more. We will talk through the lows of pain and self-doubt, and tackle the lies we hear from others and the ones we tell ourselves. We won't tiptoe around our insecurities, but instead we will face them head on as we press in to tangible action steps toward knowing and living in freedom.

With a career that is deemed successful only when it is at its loudest, I have found it increasingly difficult to find quiet. But when I do, it's worth the effort, and I know it will be for you too.

INTRODUCTION

I love interviews. And while I'm genuinely honored when interviewers ask me questions about upcoming projects or recent releases, more than anything, I enjoy listening to others' interviews. I listen to talk shows, podcasts, and YouTube shows while I'm getting ready for my day, on long drives, and while I'm spending my one to two hours a week prepping meals.

I've found that this has given me an abundance of random knowledge. I've learned about the discographies of obscure artists, the housing markets in certain areas of the United States, and all of the stories celebrities share about their kids and holiday vacations on late-night television.

My fascination with interviews started with a love for variety television shows like *Zoom* and *The Amanda Show*. I've always taken time to study transitions and structure, and to compare the delivery between improvisation and script. Growing up as an aspiring writer (and director, actress, producer), I knew the possibilities for learning through observation were endless.

As I got older and became a writer (and director, actress, producer), my observation became habitual. I watch sketches or interviews out of fascination and curiosity, but now as an adult with other tasks and obligations, I run out of time to watch the full show. And I don't want to walk around the house *listening* to comedy sketches or monologues, which are oftentimes made better by physical comedy or body language, so instead of watching, I developed the habit of listening to interviews, as I described, which I call *background interview listening*.

It's funny (and by *funny*, I mean sad) how we often don't realize the negative effects of some of our day-to-day routines. I remember with clarity when this realization came for me about my interview habit. I was sitting in a counselor's office in the spring of 2019, sharing the details of what it's like when my brain decides to run a marathon. I told her about my professional ability to overthink, which often can lead me to overact and to the late-night thoughts that keep me up.

I explained to her that because of my anxiety and OCD (obsessive-compulsive disorder), I often have obsessive thoughts that are out of my control, and my anxiety feeds into those thoughts all too well. I also told her that I am fully aware that not every imperfect aspect of my life could or should be attributed to my neurological idiosyncrasies, and that I was constantly working to differentiate the two.

I told her that as much as I love social media and the ability to do a web search or place an online shopping order and instantly have access to anything and everything I could possibly need, the instantaneous nature of our culture often added stress to my life and caused me to feel rushed, frustrated, and inadequate.

After talking a mile a minute, trying to get all of my thoughts and feelings out as quickly as possible (partially because I was feeling anxious, but mostly because I'm frugal and I like to get the most of a fifty-minute counseling session), she asked me if I ever had moments when I felt at peace.

My face lit up.

I told her all about interviews. I also told her about music, shows, and podcasts, but I especially emphasized the interviews and their ability to help me find a steady pace throughout my day. I was almost proud to be able to say that I had found a "solution" for quieting my mind and aiding my ability to focus, when she asked me a question that stopped me in my tracks:

Is your mind ever quiet without noise?

I'm not sure if that is verbatim or not, but that's certainly how I heard it and will always remember it—which I've learned is significant about conviction. It's the moment when you not only hear what you've been asked or told, but you hear your response immediately after and you know that it's not the "right" response.

My answer in this case was *no.*

In that moment I realized that in an effort to quiet my mind, my anxious thoughts, and my rushed mentality, I wasn't seeking peace or finding quiet—I was simply muting it with a different kind of noise.

As much as I had listened to interviews featuring an actor and his new film, a philanthropist and her latest mission, or an entrepreneur and her road to success, I wasn't retaining knowledge as much as I was gaining information. And in the end, what good is a significant amount of information at the expense of a hurried mind? As Jesus asks in Matthew 16:26 (and Mark 8:36),

> What good will it be for someone to gain the whole world, yet forfeit their soul?

It may seem as though I am being extreme or dramatic in saying that I shouldn't listen to interviews because it's too much noise. I want to clarify that for many people who struggle with anxiety or something similar, finding things to listen to is a helpful coping mechanism, and embracing that balance in our lives to help prevent panic attacks or other stress can be incredibly helpful. Yet when speaking in the sense of a "need" for more and more sound, the problem is not the persistent audio I hear while I put on my makeup or drive to the studio. It is the inability to sit in quiet and breathe in the silence in the presence of the One who made me, and to be just who He made me to be.

So many times we have the opportunity to face our pain, but we choose to allow noise to cover it instead.

How many times do we listen to music to escape heartbreak?

How often do we go to a movie and allow the surround sound to drown out the volume of pain in our everyday lives?

How often do we intentionally turn on a song when we're sad or angry, knowing it will only push us deeper into our sadness and despair?

So many times we have the opportunity to face our pain, but we choose to allow noise to cover it instead.

Life Tracks: Demos or Fully Produced?

I enjoy producing music. It's part of my job, but it's also a genuine hobby, and if I'm not spending time with my family, cooking, or listening to an interview, you can find me in my home studio working on a song.

Even though the guitar is my primary instrument, I usually start producing a song with either drums or piano. I find a tempo and set the metronome, oftentimes called a click track, which helps me stay on beat as I start to record. From there I supply some vocals as I finish the lyrics, gradually adding guitar, bass, and any other instruments I want.

I tend to work at a pretty fast pace. Once I have a concept in mind, my brain starts moving a mile a minute and I try to get all the melodies and rhythms recorded as soon as I can.

I almost always mess up. Like any other producer I know, I have to go back and rerecord mishaps or even new ideas, because that's simply part of the process. But occasionally I miss something. I don't realize that I hit an off note, or I simply record something differently from how I originally intended, but before I know it, I've spent hours on a song, adding instrument after instrument, track after track, and still not realizing that one little tweak has yet to be made.

It's likely I won't notice the hiccup until I go to officially record or share the song. While it's just a "work tape" or "demo" on my computer, I don't stress myself out over fully developing or producing every little moment. At this point it's something for me to listen to, continue to work on, and grow from, and nothing more. It's loud, busy, and fun, and I don't even notice that there's a random drum sound or background noise buried deep down that I probably didn't intend to be a part of the finished product. Or in some cases I *do* notice it, but since the song is only a demo, I can always go back and make adjustments later.

Sometimes we allow our lives to operate like a demo.

We experience a moment that breaks our heart, upsets us, causes anxiety, or tears us apart, and instead of choosing to right the wrongs or face the pain, we pile noise on top of the broken pieces. We add instruments, vocals, melodies, and drum pads on top of the broken piano tracks and share with the world unfinished products, hiding the depths of who we really are.

It's only the people who truly know us—and oftentimes only ourselves—who can peel away the chaos and uproar to find the fragmented pieces that we rushed over, sitting there buried beneath the noise.

A lot of times I love the demo or the acoustic, artist-interview interpretation of a song more than I like the one that charts on the radio. I would rather my favorite artist sing in my living room than hear the fully produced and perfected track through my headphones. It's imperfect and complex and maybe even a little off-key, but it reflects the reality of life and is far more relatable than anything perfectly tuned.

More important, God isn't looking for us to be perfect. He has no interest in us pretending that our days or minds or hearts exist without flaw. But He *is* interested in us bringing those flaws to Him. He is in the business of righting wrongs, mending hurting hearts, and putting broken pieces back together.

So why do we hide our brokenness?

Why do we bury our pain?
Why do we cover up our hurt?

For many of us, when we face pain, everything shuts down. When we find out that our dream job or school is out of reach . . . when we go through a breakup . . . when someone takes advantage of us physically, emotionally, or sexually . . . when we can't resolve an argument with someone we love . . . when we let down the person who has continually believed in us . . . when we break another's heart . . . when we hear of the death of a loved one—it feels silent. It feels like the world around us has stopped, and for a moment, it's only us—and so much uneasy quiet.

We face this every day if we're battling anxious thoughts or even a diagnosis of anxiety. We are triggered by a thought, a smell, or even a sound that takes us back to the hopeless and daunting feeling of being absolutely alone.

When we're faced with such quiet, we have only two options:

We can fill the room and fill our heads with countless sounds and noise to drown out the pain that we don't want to face,

OR

We can find refuge and maybe even strength, allowing quiet to be more than the absence of noise and to be truly the epitome of peace.

We can enjoy the imperfect demos as well as the impeccably produced songs, allowing our lives to dance even while flawed and broken, as we rush to the feet of the perfect One who mends all.

I will forever love music, podcasts, and interviews. I will listen to piano ballads when I'm in my feelings, dance to upbeat songs when I'm in a good mood, and crave a good interview when I want to learn something new.

Simultaneously, I will actively seek *quiet*. I will embrace the moments that make me feel weak and allow my mind to be pursued by the One who does His best work *in* my weakness.

And throughout this book, I'll invite you to join me. There will be moments filled with memories of when I found quiet, some poems, and strategies.

Together, we'll find the balance of beautiful noise that carries us to places we've never been, while choosing to face the fear of the simpler times when quiet becomes our fortitude.

We'll have moments of joy and laughter as well as challenges and convictions. But through it all we will grow and learn on a crazy, exciting, and resilient journey to finding quiet.

—Jamie Grace

one

The Toll of Daily Anxious Thoughts

When I was seven, I made a decision to love Jesus for the rest of my life.

When I was eleven, I was diagnosed with anxiety (as well as Tourette Syndrome, obsessive-compulsive disorder, and attention-deficit/hyperactivity disorder).

I daily experience an exceptional amount of anxiety.

I daily experience an exceptional amount of faith.

Every day I struggle with the fear of allowing the wrong side to win.

My faith tells me that anything is possible. It tells me to allow my Creator's strength to be made perfect in my weaknesses. It tells me that while I am not perfect, my Creator doesn't make mistakes. I am loved as I am. Yet I am in need of perfect grace to carry me. The grace is available—new mercies every day. And if beauty were a sound, my faith would be the loudest.

But anxiety's voice is speaking too.

My anxiety tells me that silence and uncertainty mean I am not loved. It tells me that if I make a mistake, I should replay it until I make a new mistake that's worse—and then I will start replaying that one. But the only thing that happens is a never-ending cycle of ruminating over what I've done wrong or what I said that was awkward, instead of extending even a small amount of grace to myself. Anxiety tells me that people might not like me—a problem that is *my* responsibility (it's not) and needs to be solved right away (it doesn't). It tells me that I can't get out of bed sometimes, so I stay there. Or that I can't spend time with my friends (for no reason), so I cancel. It leaves me in utter panic that if I go out or leave my room, I am making a big mistake.

It tells me that if I text someone back right away I seem too anxious, but if I wait too long they must think I don't care enough. So I leave my texts unread for weeks, often feeling my breathing speed up at the idea of apologizing for taking so long to get back to them. I'm convinced that they believe I've gotten "too famous" or simply don't care, so I stare at the words, hoping for relief until I eventually find the courage to say something. Anything.

Usually their response is incredibly chill. But I can find a way to overanalyze that too.

It's difficult to understand because it's hard to explain. I've spent most of my adult life trying to figure out the line between my clinically diagnosed anxiety and my character flaws and emotional weaknesses—and how in the world I should recover.

I tried medication.

I was pretty heavily medicated from ages nine through fifteen. My tics from Tourette's were becoming increasingly aggressive and violent as my legs flailed and kicked whoever was standing by, or my neck jerked while I was in the car and my head slammed into the rear door window. In an effort to keep me safe, my parents and I decided together that I should try medication, but the results were not worth the side effects. The goal of the medication was to calm my tics down, but as a result, I became sluggish and exhausted and lacked the drive or motivation to do much of anything. In the end, it made sense to avoid those medications altogether.

I tried to pray.

I tried the soft, sweet prayers where I talked to Jesus like I'm on a smoothie date with my best friend. It's almost like we walked into a local juice bar and placed our orders of Krazy Kale Blast and Strawberry Banana Bananza to sit down and quietly talk through our differences. I would politely and calmly say, "Jesus, I want to talk about my illness," and our conversation would continue from there. I have humbly requested to be delivered from a lifestyle of worry and repetitive, often self-deprecating, thoughts.

I tried talking to Him like He was a best friend who stabbed me in the back, but not in the metaphorical sense. The anger and frustration of feeling betrayed, misled, and manipulated built inside of me as I tried to understand how and why the One I trusted most would take something from me—my peace, my joy—and not give it back. I have screamed, yelled, and possibly been too proud, nearly demanding freedom. I have felt moments of relief. Moments of peace. But my daily battle is still being fought.

I tried medication—again.

In my early twenties, I was working too much. I love my job and would never trade it, but I was a full-time college student who was touring five days a week, as well as writing and creating a record on my off days. I met with my neurologist, whom I hadn't seen since I was fifteen, and we decided that a low dose of antidepressants might be helpful. It was, for a season. But that season didn't last forever.

I tried counseling.

My alma mater required all counseling majors (which I was for a semester) to go to at least one session with the campus counselor. I was terrified at first. But when I realized that I could sit across from someone and talk through *all* of my over-analyzations (fifty minutes' worth, anyway) and she was legally obligated to try to help *and* to keep it all a secret? I was overwhelmed with gratitude and desperately wanted her to be my new friend. After our session I even tried friending her on Facebook—until she told me that counselors and clients couldn't be friends like that. I felt embarrassed and awkward, and the humiliation and insecurity sent me into a few days of isolation and I avoided her office at all costs. #anxiety

In 2016 I found a counselor who walked with me through heavy pain and anger. I was happy to find hope again after moments of thinking it had been lost. We met weekly for a few months, and on two or three occasions we even met twice a week. She asked thought-provoking questions that led me to want to grow spiritually and emotionally, and walked me through steps to make those changes. She helped me understand words like *trauma* and *victim*, and helped me learn how to not only receive grace from God and extend it to others, but to extend it to myself too.

A year after I met her, I moved from Atlanta to Los Angeles and didn't want to face the anxiety of trying to find a new person to trust. It was so challenging that it was nearly a year of living on the West Coast before I found a new counselor. My first meeting with him was exceptional. He asked me questions about myself and shared quite a bit about his process. I went back the second week, confident about digging a little deeper, when about halfway through the session he said something that counteracted with my faith. It was unrelated to both our session and my story, but I shut down. I never went back.

In 2019, another year later, I finally pursued counseling again. And much like my Atlanta sessions, it has now become a weekly source of encouragement, support, accountability, and even laughter. I enjoy my counselor, our meetings, and even her office and the noise machine in the hallway. And while I don't expect to ever live a perfect life, I still have moments of anxiety that are further from my own expectations.

I'm able to hear the voice of reason and rationality, and I want to live a life where it speaks louder than fear and doubt.

I want to live a life free from overthinking. I want to be able to say what I believe should be said, live as I have been called to live, and love others the way I believe we all deserve to be loved, without picking things apart. I want to be able to have conversations without being stuck on the way I said hello, and watch a movie with my family without the fear that their silence (remember, we're watching a movie) means they're upset with me.

I'm able to hear the voice of reason and rationality, and I want to live a life where it speaks louder than fear and doubt.

Breaking Point

One day when my husband, Aaron, came home, about two months into our marriage, I broke down crying the second he walked through the door. It was only the second time it had happened since we got married (note: I'm currently worrying what you think of me as I'm typing, and trying to convince myself I shouldn't delete this paragraph), which would seem like an improvement compared with previous seasons in my life, when I would have breakdowns almost every day. But looking back, I realized I had settled on a new way of coping—instead of counseling, prayer, and/or medication, I had begun bottling up all of my tiny feelings until they became a big pile of feelings that simply couldn't be bottled anymore.

For weeks, I had taken every small alert in my head and buried it. I hadn't talked about anything because of the fear of how I would be perceived. I was afraid to speak up because I was nervous of what Aaron would say if I needed to talk for fifteen minutes about something incredibly random, off-topic, and analytical just to calm myself down. So instead, I carried around irrational fear until a day when it was just too heavy.

This day's spiral had started with a phone conversation with my mom, which led to my dad joining on speaker. They were attempting to reassure me that I was overthinking a small detail, but anxiety assured me that panic was the only option. When Aaron walked in the front door that day, I broke down. I cried. I ranted. I sobbed. I could barely catch my breath while trying to explain all of the seemingly minuscule stresses that had built into this massive breaking point.

I remember him asking me if there was anything he could say, do, or even not say or do. I told him there wasn't anything for him to do, and I didn't know how to calm down or stop my tears. So he simply asked if he could sit with me until I would be ready to talk, and hold me, so I didn't have to cry alone. I said yes. And that's exactly what we did.

While there is no such thing as a perfect human, I know that Aaron is the perfect one for me (#cheese), because in that moment, instead of judging me or making me feel worse, he decided to sit with me and be the physical representation of love and support that I needed.

Fear, Truth, and the Result

My parents tell me that I've repeated this cycle since I was a kid. I had anxiety about personal issues like what to wear to a friend's house or who I should or shouldn't invite to my birthday party. And sometimes issues that were bigger than I weighed me down and kept me up at night as I felt overwhelmed by the fact that I wasn't old enough to be a foster mom or that I didn't know exactly how to end homelessness in America. I would start to overthink, overanalyze, and even self-deprecate, to the point that my anxious thoughts became anxious feelings, and I would find myself falling onto the couch or into my parents' arms, crying, panicking, and worrying.

My parents have told me these stories, and many of them I remember for myself. Every new life change, whether good or bad, brings about new anxieties and new learning curves. But no matter how great the classroom, I don't always like the lesson.

It's a terrible habit to bury your pain until it eventually overflows. So in the spirit of being a human who seems to thrive on repetitiveness, I've begun to create new habits for myself in an effort to find healing:

I make a choice to say three things to talk myself back from whatever downward spiral my mind is attempting to chase:

1. My greatest fear
2. What I know
3. The truth

Fear, What I Know & the Truth

I was afraid he would judge me.
I knew he wouldn't judge me.
He didn't judge me.

I was afraid he would think I'm too much.
I know he doesn't think I'm too much.
He doesn't think I'm too much.

I was afraid he would seem frustrated.
I knew he wouldn't seem frustrated.
He wasn't frustrated.

I know the truth.
I have a faith in the truth.
I just have anxiety too.

I don't know what my life without anxiety and OCD would look like. I don't know what the future for an overactive mind looks like. I don't know when I'll have a bad day of overthinking again or if I've reached the worst of it. I don't know if this is all mind, some emotions, mostly personality, a sprinkle of neurological abnormalities, or a mixture of it all (likely the latter).

But I do know that I can't live like this. With a diagnosis of asthma, which requires me to have a prescription nebulizer, I know I cannot be trapped in my own mind, believing that I need an inhaler more than my actual lungs.

FINDING QUIET

My earliest memories are loud, ambient, and full of racing and anxious thoughts. They are flooded with fear and insecurity. Low self-esteem. Significant self-doubt.

Except when they're not.

I *do* have peaceful memories: When I was five and sang at our school's graduation. When I was six and sang at the pavilion in Stone Mountain. When I was seven and I sang along with my mom while she led worship. This list goes on.

I like the way it feels to sing. But more than that, I like to know that the words I'm sharing just might help someone get through the week, the day—the moment. And maybe, if I really press in to what it means to feel, the words can reach me too.

The joy in writing and sharing what's on my mind is one of the greatest thrills in life. Singing, talking, creating a video, dancing, writing . . . I get anxious because I'm ready to share the next word, yet I'm at peace because I get to.

And that's what brings us here. My journey of finding and accepting peace as much as I can. The great, the challenging, and the everywhere in between of finding quiet in the midst of diagnosed anxiety, overthinking, and overanalyzing.

It's easy to believe that everything will be okay when everything is okay. It's the moments when we feel like everything is crumbling before us . . . that faith proves just how powerful it can be.

And whether or not you have clinically diagnosed anxiety or deal with any other trace or form of anxious or racing thoughts, I hope you know that it's okay to feel that way and still have faith. Faith that you can *still* have joy. Faith that you can *still* have a song to sing—even if you're not a good singer. ☺

If we're being honest, our faith *during* these times is what can show us just how powerful faith truly is. It's easy to believe that everything will be okay when everything is okay. It's the moments when we feel like everything is crumbling before us and completely falling apart that *faith* proves just how powerful it can be.

We're going to get through this.

We're not going to pretend that a book or a song or any earthly treasure can lead us to any version of a perfect life. But we are going to work hard to find hope and support as we navigate toward the definition of *quiet* and our choice to embrace it.

On our journey to finding quiet, here are three reminders that can help us along the way:

1. **You are not alone.** You might *feel* alone because you can't hear other people's thoughts and insecurities, but other people are afraid that they are being judged too. There are other people who are scared about the future or regretful about the past, and there are so many people who are praying for peace.

2. **Not everyone is going to understand, and that's okay.** You can still have faith that the right people will be placed in your life at the right time. Even people like Job didn't get the support from his friends that he thought he would, and Jesus himself was let down by people close to Him. This is all a part of life, but it doesn't mean that you can't have faith that there *will* be people you can count on.

3. **It's okay to ask for help.** You are not alone—you do not have to walk through this alone— and that may mean that you have to take the first step toward building community. I'm grateful for my family and their choice to continually invest in me. I also have to make the choice to go to my counselor's office, to be honest with my medical team if I feel like I'm having a setback, and to be transparent with my mentor and friends when issues arise.

We won't allow anxious thoughts to take our peace hostage.

We won't allow anxiety to captivate our rest.

We won't allow overthinking and over-analyzation to dictate who we are.

We will find quiet.

Oftentimes we will have to seek it out more than once, pursuing it again and again. There may even be times when peace will coexist with pain, and rest will seem to collide with our tears and sleepless nights. But we have come too far and invested too much to give up now.

We will persist.

We will press on.

We will fight and we will surrender.

Truth. 09.22.19

*I choose to let truth have the final word, even though lies
    are easier to believe.*

*I fight in a daily battle against anxiety that tells me that
    I'm not enough.*

I'm not beautiful.

I'm not successful.

My voice doesn't matter and my words don't hold value.

*And I can't even say that anxiety says that I'm not loved
    and cherished. Because anxiety takes a step further
    into my insecurities and says I'm not even able to be
    loved. I'm not even capable of giving love.*

*I should hang up my coat or throw in the towel or give
    up the hope of hoping to matter because I am far from*

loveable, not even decent, just breath and bones with
density decreasing moment by moment each minute
of the day every second of every hour I hear my mind
say just stay in bed, don't get up, why would you add
to the world?

You're a burden, you're too much, you're too cliché—
rhyming girl with world.
You have nothing to offer.
You have nothing to say.
The songs they liked were a onetime thing. The videos will
fade, just stay in bed, don't get up.

Don't brush your hair, don't eat, don't sleep, just stare at
the wall and think about the most awkward things
you've said.
Ruminate over the worst parts of your day.
Start a cycle of pain, fear, and doubt where you can't
function or process freedom or being freed from the
weight that's on you heavier than shame, heavier than
pain because it bears the reality of every negativity ever
named.

Don't text your friends.
Give it weeks at a time.
Don't answer your phone.
Let it ring, but push that little button so it rings on silent
so people think you're busy changing the world and
writing songs when you're really in a dark, quiet room
staring at a wall.

I fight.
Some would say to fight is to be free from all pain. But
the reality is my fight is the ability to see pain. To see

*my brokenness broken before a battle every day, where
I choose to let truth have the final say. I'm not asking
my pain to never exist because without disgust, beauty
could never exist. Without pain, I wouldn't understand
healing and without being weighed down I couldn't
appreciate freedom.*

*So when my mind starts to wander and my thoughts
start to scream, I let them have their moment to open
the show because this gig doesn't pay a thing. Not
my time, not my attention, not even lousy applause, I
write down the exact lies that my mind wants to tell
and I let truth step up to the mic and be the headliner.*
*Because my mind says that I'm not enough. But truth
says that I don't have to be. Because I was made by the
epitome of enough for me and He does His best work
when I am weak.*
*My mind says I'm not beautiful and I'm too big and too
weird. But truth says there's something wonderfully
made about me, and I can't get my truth from a scale
or a mirror.*
*My mind says I talk too much and I should just be quiet.
But truth says what if there's a new season that could
change the world? What if your story is the pilot?*
What if our minds are the biggest liars?
*Somewhere between anxiety, depression, and our
character flaws? What if they're not yet trained to
always tell us what we need so instead all we hear are
despicable, disgusting things?*
*And what if instead of being consumed with the fix, we
sat in the hurt, the pain and the sick. We wrote down*

the untruths and the doubts and the worst and we
choose in a moment to let truth have the final word.
Even when lies are easier to believe. When sad songs are
more fun and isolation more convenient. Or even
when it's painful to break down day after day but
somehow it's easier than speaking up and asking for
help. When panic attacks are easier to understand
than peace even though they tear us apart and leave us
feeling weaker than the moment we started.

I fight a daily battle.
And I make a daily choice.

In the discombobulated truth that is my world, when I
don't always believe it and even when I don't know
how, I choose to let truth have the final word.

two

The Noise of Feelings

I have an odd relationship with feelings. I used to joke about being "emotionally constipated" and desiring a good, sad movie to get all of those tears out. And when a friend is going through a painful situation or facing issues with their life choices or family, I take pride in being the one they trust to map out the issues from day one and help them navigate through every twist and turn.

I love feelings . . . or so I thought.

I've recently come to realize that I only love feeling things when it's "okay" for me to feel them. For example, it's okay to feel sad watching a sad movie because clearly the writers were trying to connect with the viewer in that way. And it's okay to feel empathetic with a friend when they're facing a difficult time, because they need you. But if I ever feel upset or confused and I can't seem to find a reason, I tend to detach from feeling anything, as though my feelings need to be justified.

Realistically, there's no difference in feelings. There are no justified or unjustified feelings. Feelings simply *are*. You can feel mad, sad, happy, confused, overwhelmed, excited, and obviously so much more. But when it comes to my own personal feelings, I have a hard time accepting that.

Imagine two people are in an argument.

In my mind, if the words or actions of Person 1 hurt the feelings of Person 2, then Person 2's hurt feelings are okay—until Person 1 has apologized. Once Person 1 has genuinely said that they are sorry, or it's come to the surface that it wasn't intentional, Person 2 needs to move on.

But that's not realistic! In some scenarios, Person 1 may apologize, but Person 2 may still be hurt. And if you were Person 2, I would make sure to tell you this! But if *I* am Person 2? Then it doesn't apply.

I've somehow convinced myself that everyone else in the world is allowed to feel hurt, pain, insecurity, and even disgust no matter what. Your feelings are your feelings and they are a part of your healing and recovery.

Why?

Because I love feelings.

But only until I have to *really* feel them.

My mom is sick. She was born with a condition that limits her physical mobility. It often makes her sad, and as her family members who love and care about her, we deal with those feelings too. There are days when I can remind my mom that it's okay to feel hurt. I reassure my dad that heartache for her pain is real and okay. My sister . . . her husband . . . my husband

. . . whatever feelings they have when they see my mom struggling are okay. The feelings are not directed at my mom. The feelings are not wrong. The feelings simply *are*.

I, however, am not allowed to have those feelings. It's not my mom's fault that she's sick, so if I feel hurt or sad or broken or even mad or upset, it leads to shame. It brings about guilt. I feel weak. I feel incapable. I feel like I am attacking my mom for something that is out of her control. I can't feel those things. I need to feel only good things.

Why?

A member of my extended family said some hurtful things to me, and my heart was broken, nearly destroyed. I shared the scenarios with close friends and family, asking, "Is it okay that I'm mad?" "Does it make sense that I'm angry?" It was as though I had to get permission to feel. I have this constant need and desire to do what's right, to feel right, which isn't inherently bad until I acknowledge that there's no way to feel "right." Feelings just are.

I don't think anyone caught on to my need for permission, but they always granted it. I wasn't being irrational—I was simply feeling.

In this situation, I chose to speak to my family member about their hurtful words and my feelings. That person denied their actions, which caused me to feel anxious and confused and angry. Furious. So I took some time to sort through the new feelings (also a panic attack and weeks of isolation) to see what I needed to do next.

I didn't do anything. My family member later apologized. And while it wasn't the apology I was anticipating or maybe had hoped for, I chose to forgive. I was able to see past the actions and into the root of this person's "why." I was able to process the cliché wrapped in truth that "hurt people hurt people" and understand that this person's choices had nothing to do with me, but were rooted in the pain they were facing. Maybe they have a weird relationship with their feelings too.

It seems like the story should wrap up here. That it should be over. We tie a ribbon on our recovery and move on—but I don't. All because, in my way of thinking, I'm no longer allowed to feel: they apologized; I forgave them.

So why do I still feel a sting when I am reminded of what happened? Why do I still feel pain when I hear that person's name? Why do I still feel triggered when we talk? Does this mean my forgiveness has been undone or maybe wasn't done at all? Am I not doing things the right way?

If this were anyone else's story, I would tell them that it's because feelings are real. I would tell them that it's okay to forgive someone, move past the situation, and still acknowledge that feelings simply are and will be. I would tell them that healing won't happen overnight, and that their feelings are crucial to their recovery.

So feel.

Please feel.

Because the only way you can begin to heal is to acknowledge that there's something that needs healing. The only way to embrace freedom is to recognize that in some way, you've been bound. The only way to find strength is to realize that you are weak. So as we're pursuing freedom and healing, we *have* to feel the things that break us and make us feel weak.

We may want to prove that we're strong and whole, capable of pushing beyond any negative thought or feeling on our own, but we're not. God is the only One whose strength is unmatched and whose track record is undefeated. And once we feel the things we may want to avoid, we increase our chances of pressing in to the Source that provides the results we crave.

Allowing Myself to Feel

If this were anyone else's story, I would have the words, songs, poems, and paragraphs to compile in an email. A ten-step process to healing and recovery.

But it is not anyone else's story; it is mine. And for some reason my feelings just aren't able to *be*.

But what I am learning is that I am not alone in struggling to find solutions for my feelings so I can justify them and put them away. A lot of people feel this way. It's easier to help others than to realize we need help ourselves.

It's kind of like organizing someone else's stuff (which is one of my favorite activities, by the way). If you give me the option to go to the mall with an unlimited budget to buy *anything* I want, or go to the house where five kids under five live and reorganize their home, I would gladly choose the latter.

> *I am not alone in struggling to find solutions for my feelings so I can justify them and put them away. . . . It's easier to help others than to realize we need help ourselves.*

While I love organizing things in my own home, I would much rather help someone else color-coordinate the shirts in their closet and decide where every bowl and plate should go in the kitchen cabinets. And don't get me started on the pantry! I have no idea why I find it cathartic to organize cans and seasonings alphabetically, but I do. I have done this for friends and family members more times than I can count.

I remember when I was a few months pregnant and my sister suggested I join a mom-group online, made up of women who were all due around the same time I was. It was a great idea, as I read stories that related to my own and shared some of the aspects of my own life. However, there was one post in particular that made me feel very worried, and as I sit here now with a six-month-old, I can still remember it vividly.

It was a meme about organizing your child's room. The first half showed the *Before the Baby Arrives*, with perfectly organized and color-coordinated dressers, shelves, and closet space. Then it showed the *After the Baby Arrives*, where everything was out of place and nothing was where it should be. The post flooded with likes and comments, sharing how it was relatable and hilarious, and how the first-time moms (like me) would soon understand.

As an artist living out the cliché, my studio is usually a mess. Since I am an avid home cook, our kitchen counters can often be crowded with my containers and cookbooks. But as a bedroom-organizing aficionado, I felt attacked! I definitely laughed out loud because the meme was hilarious, but I simultaneously felt so much nervousness as I hoped that specific scenario would not represent my life.

My daughter's dressers have a total of nine drawers. Before Isabella was born, there were very specific places for every onesie (organized by style and size), sleeper, swaddle, diaper, and binky, as well as the headbands and books that wouldn't fit on their respective shelves. There was even a drawer for all of the feeding and pumping supplies, with separate sections within that drawer for every stage of her first year.

In her closet, all of the dressier clothes were hanging and organized from right to left, newborn to 2T. Between my parents, myself, and my husband, we can't help but buy her cute things when they're on sale, even if she can't wear them for two years. Even so, I keep them in her closet. When she grows out of one section, I pack it away and move everything over a few inches to the right, so her updated size is right in front of me.

I am determined to fight the meme. Ha! I love organization, I love structure, and I consider it a privilege to be able to help implement that into someone else's life for ease and comfort— even if my daughter is too young to appreciate it just yet.

But as much as I love organizing for everyone else, I have had to learn how to make room to organize my own stuff. When it comes to helping others, it's not really a choice I make but rather something I just *do.* But when it comes to sorting out things for myself, it's a conscious decision and choice I have to make that I *am* allowed to have that structure for myself.

As ironic as it might sound, there's something freeing about structure. There's a breath of fresh air I subconsciously breathe when I make the choice to find time for quieting the disarray— whether audible or physical—in my life.

Recently I decided to organize all my production goals into a hot-pink binder. (Something about the bright color motivates me to be creative!) The binder is organized by the music I'm producing for myself and others, songs I'm working on, and the schedule of my podcast for the coming weeks. For the podcasts I produce, I have everything organized on Excel sheets.

If I'm honest, I'm really proud of my systems. It gives me a place to apply my desire for structure and my passion for organization without forcing myself to put that same system in place for my feelings.

It has taught me that even though it's hard to go to an emotional place and give myself permission to feel those messy and unorganized feelings, when I *do* actually bravely tackle working through it, I feel better. I'm no longer "emotionally constipated" when it's all out. I feel *free*.

Jesus Felt

One of my favorite verses in the Bible is when Jesus is on the cross. Matthew 27:46 recounts Jesus crying out "*Eli, Eli, lema sabachthani?*" which translates to "My God, my God, why have you forsaken me?"

I love this moment of deep emotion from the Savior of the world. When Jesus was in deep pain after all of the rejection and betrayal He experienced, He expressed His feelings. While there is only a brief documentation of this moment—and Jesus certainly doesn't sit in the hurt for long—He *still* had feelings, and He had no shame in expressing that pain.

Not only do I desire to be more like Jesus in the moments when He extends grace and mercy, I also choose to strive to be like Him in the moment He embraced pain too.

Yet even through those agonizing hours and days following the crucifixion, there was still the promise of the resurrection. Jesus faced something beyond what we can understand. He was ridiculed, mocked, spat on, beaten, abused, and *then* hung on a cross, where He died a brutal and gruesome death. But the whole situation was still in God's hands and had a moment (literally *the moment* when He rose from the dead) of resolve in the end.

Matthew 27:46 gives me hope. It reminds me that our feelings that seem so messy at times are still wrapped in God's promises. The feelings that I oftentimes worry shouldn't exist are valid and they won't last, but if I press in to them, through them, His promises will be there on the other side.

When Jesus asked, "Why have you forsaken me?" He was still Jesus. He was still fully aware of God's plan and knew that there would be the most incredible miracle in the end. Yet He took that moment to feel and to express it.

I want to challenge us to do the same. While we don't know the details of tomorrow, we know for a fact that God has not failed us and will not forsake us (Deuteronomy 31:6). We know that God has a plan, and our present is not indicative of what He has in store for the future (Jeremiah 29:11).

So when we face adversity yet want to remain hopeful for the future, let's not forget to sit in the moments that linger in the middle.

In the feelings.

Our goal isn't to become so set in our feelings that we lose sight of how to hope. But we don't want to become so anxious for hope that we don't have time for the grief that led us there.

It's Okay to Feel

I recently had a challenging moment in my life show up in a way I would have never expected. While I didn't want to have to face it, I was glad that it just so happened to be right before a session with my counselor. (I will say that one of the greatest gifts I have found during the challenges in life is when they happen just before lunch with a mentor or a session with a solid counselor.)

As I sat there sharing all the details of the situation, my counselor asked a question that she had not asked me up until this point, yet one that is a variation of *the* counselor's question:

"How are you feeling?"

I stared at her in silence.

In my efforts to find a solution to make everyone happy . . .

In my efforts to figure out the steps to remain positive . . .

In my efforts to be better . . . pursue better . . . extend and receive grace . . .

I had forgotten to feel.

I had jumped from offense to recovery with no pain in between, and I was falling apart. I felt anxious, uptight, and like a ticking time bomb that would explode at any moment. The tenseness brought on by my unconscious choice not to feel was taking over, and if it hadn't been for someone genuinely asking me, "How are you feeling?" I don't know when or how I would have stopped to discover the answer.

Interestingly enough, the answer didn't come right away. We sat in silence for a moment, and I felt more perplexed than I had in a while. It wasn't that I had forgotten to feel, but I had forgotten that I *could* feel. But I didn't even know where to start processing my feelings. So I slowly but surely started going through the possible answers until I landed on the ones that resonated with me in that moment.

In the most beautiful breakdown of exploring all seasons, Ecclesiastes 3:4 describes "a time to weep and a time to laugh." I love to laugh. And I genuinely love the moments when I let myself feel. But I have to make it a daily reminder to push past the guilt that often coincides with feelings, and embrace the freedom that also comes when I feel.

A woman wrote in to my podcast, asking if it was okay that she wasn't yet ready to date. Her husband had passed away and she was now a widow and a single mom. She was feeling pressure because the women at her church said it was time for her to date and wanted to set her up with men, but she wasn't ready.

She asked if it was okay that she still loved her husband, missed him, and didn't feel like she was ready to move on. She was grieving the loss of the most important man in her life, but because of the pressure from other people, she began to doubt if she was doing the right thing. She was overwhelmed and frustrated that maybe, just maybe, she wasn't feeling the way she "should."

> *I have to make it a daily reminder to push past the guilt that often coincides with feelings, and embrace the freedom that also comes when I feel.*

FINDING QUIET

Know this: Wisdom is needed. It's imperative that we surround ourselves with wise men and women who will give us godly counsel both when we ask for it and when we don't. It's also important that we become wise men and women, seeking out wisdom in an effort to grow personally and to invest in the lives of others.

But don't ever allow anyone else's concept of the ideal situation to become the pressure in your own life, masquerading as wisdom. There are many accounts throughout the Bible—the ultimate source of wisdom and counsel—that would validate these four words:

It's okay to feel.

It is also natural if

- it takes time to move on.
- it takes time to figure things out.
- you need to feel a little longer than anticipated.
- you need to feel a little deeper than you thought.
- you're still heartbroken after the breakup.
- you're still tired of being single.
- you feel angry because someone betrayed your trust.
- you feel discouraged after a rough semester.
- you feel lonely, even at church.
- you feel confused by the mixed signals of the person you've been texting.
- you feel shame because of what you've done in the past.
- you feel anxious about the future.
- you feel overwhelmed by your job.
- you feel overwhelmed as a parent.

Our feelings are, but Jesus is more.
There is still hope.
There is always the resurrection.

three

Fixing Things

I have vivid memories of movie nights at our house. We didn't watch a ton of television growing up, but when we did, it usually brought the entire family together and had been on our calendar for days in advance. My mom would bring dinner into the living room while my sister and I picked out what movie to watch. Even though we knew how to work the DVD player (er, VHS), running it was always one of those "dad jobs." He's an electrician by trade, and anything with a lightbulb or a power button is right up his alley.

Whenever we watched a movie together, it was almost like a day at work for my dad. He always rigged up a high-tech surround-sound system so we could hear every word and onomatopoeia in the film. Because we weren't a well-off family (which I have no shame in), it meant that *our* surround-sound system had a homemade element.

We were (and proudly still are) professional secondhand shoppers, so almost everything in our living room was used. The speakers were all different brands and most of the remote controls were universal ones that somehow occasionally got reprogrammed. The wires weren't always the most stable, so the audio wasn't consistent, but we weren't the complaining type. In our minds, we had an incredible home theater system by Dad, and an amazing dine-in experience by Mom. My sister and I were living the dream.

As you might suspect, this called for a lot of fixing. More often than not, my dad would end up behind the TV, under a shelf, or wherever, rewiring, readjusting, or reprogramming something. We were content with watching the movie on full screen, but nope—Dad wanted us to see the full effect in wide screen. We were content with the audio coming from under the TV, but nope—he wouldn't have wired speakers behind us if he didn't want the sound to come from all around.

There were many nights when our movie was delayed twenty or thirty minutes because Dad insisted on fixing. I'm not trying to paint us as the most well-behaved children, but we didn't have a problem waiting it out. We just got a head start on dinner and waited for him to fix it. Because that's what he always did. Dad always fixed things.

I could spend hours talking about all the things my dad and mom fixed. From electrical disasters to emotional messes, they fix things.

I remember spending most Wednesday nights after Bible study waiting on the church pews with my sister as we heard our parents counsel a couple in the next room. The couple would walk in looking a little down, or even genuinely frustrated, but an hour or two later, many would walk out smiling, as though they had just figured something out. And sometimes they would even be laughing.

When my sister, Morgan, and I got into any kind of debate or disagreement, whether it was about which doll belonged to whom or who *actually* won a board game, our parents would want to fix it. They would help us navigate through the tough conversations to make sure that we didn't harbor our frustration but instead worked through it right then and there.

As an adult, I can look back and also see situations where they stepped away and allowed us to grow on our own, or simply couldn't fix it so they didn't continue to try. But I always had a difficult time deciphering the choices they made in these cases and instead began to put *fixing* on a pedestal.

I Can't Fix Everything

A lot of my complexities are rooted in my desire to see people happy, and devastation when things go wrong. I love when people smile, and I can't take it when they don't, but the result is not a complete train wreck. The need (er, *want*) to solve every issue and fix every problem can push me to show love to others and reach out as a friend.

When my friends go through a breakup or have a really bad date, I am most often one of the first calls they make. I consider it a privilege that they know that 7 a.m. isn't too early and 4 a.m isn't too late. When my friends are in the valley and need someone to be there, I'm there. And even if they don't need advice or someone to "fix it," I know that by listening or simply sitting with them, I am fortunate to be a part of their understanding that they're not alone.

I've even carried this into my concerts. I know, music concerts are a blast for most people, but one day I looked out into the crowd and saw that there were some dads who came *only* because their daughters wanted to. While I do have male fans young and old, I was noticing an increase in dads who looked like they were counting down the number of songs to gauge how much longer the show might be. So I made it my goal to make *everyone* smile at my shows at least once.

To get the dads to smile, I actually ended up writing a song called "The Dad Song." I routinely play it halfway through my shows—just when dads might be starting to lose interest. I didn't like the idea of them sitting through an hour and a half of something they probably wouldn't naturally attend, so I carved out approximately four minutes to "fix" the problem, in a sarcastic yet sincere way, and to thank them for their time.

When I'm meeting people after a show, I always look for the kid standing in line who doesn't look like they have any friends, because that kid was me. I remember what it's like to go through an autograph line with your youth group, knowing that everyone else planned what to say and what to get signed, and feeling that you'll be left out.

I make it a point to see that everyone who comes through my line, especially those who may seem detached and insecure, feels welcome and loved. I know I can't fix the situations that may follow them home, but even if only for a moment, I want them to know there's someone who sees them and truly cares.

I hope that compassion is something that both leads and follows me every day. I hope that my desire to extend love and grace, often under the mask of fixing, continues to be the way that I operate in my marriage and as a mom, daughter, sister, and friend.

However, I am constantly aware of the fact that the need to fix can easily get out of hand. What can seem like a strength can become one of my greatest weaknesses when I allow it to translate into feelings of not being "enough" if I can't find, create, or even be the cure.

When I was a teenager, one of my friends posted some things on social media that were both promiscuous and illegal. While concerned, I toiled for months over what I should say and how I should say it. I didn't want to be the friend to rat her out, but I didn't want to stand by silently either. The truth eventually came out, and she was confronted by her family, who desperately wanted answers.

> *What can seem like a strength can become one of my greatest weaknesses when I allow it to translate into feelings of not being "enough" if I can't find, create, or even be the cure.*

Late one night, I received a phone call from my friend. She told me about the "intervention" and asked if I could come over right away.

I got in my car with tears in my eyes. I had spent months worried that she could end up further involved with the wrong crowd, or even worse, in trouble with the law. But I knew that this night would end in tears and reconciliation, and maybe even the promise to put everything in the past and leave it there. I know that rehabilitation and healing doesn't happen overnight, and I didn't anticipate perfection or immediate freedom, but I knew there was a problem and that problems should be fixed. So I hopped into my car, hurting and hopeful, and drove until I arrived at her house.

The remainder of the evening was quiet and somewhat eerie. Anger, disgust, confusion, and pain weighed heavy in the room, yet no one's voice was raised. Every word spoken was soft and gentle, yet laced with the inner battle of how to express yourself without exposing your pride. And it would seem that because the conversations were controlled, compromise and change were on the rise. But as I would find out the next day and for days and weeks to come, change was nowhere in sight.

At minimum, the push to ending her illegal behavior was mutually agreed upon, yet her dangerous and risky choices that added fuel to the flames were not off the table, and everyone knew it.

I tried as hard as I could to offer support and encouragement, and to champion my friend however she needed. I offered to check in more often or to check in less, but no matter what I said or did, it was either too much or not enough. I prayed, I cried, and I hoped for better for her—someone whose talent was exceptional and whose potential was unmatched. But in the end, it wasn't received at all, and ultimately, I lost all communication with one of my closest friends.

God Is the True Fixer

God fixes things. Always. Whether those fixes are seen on earth or in heaven, He will always remain the greatest *fixer* there ever was and ever will be. I know it may sound cheesy or cliché, but it's simply who He is.

This is why I love the book of Job. Job's story starts off beautifully, as the Bible describes who he is, all that he is blessed with, and his love for and choice to pursue God. Then Job's faith is tested. Job loses everything, including his family, and finds himself alone. Even when friends do come and visit, it turns out their intentions are impure and their advice is misleading.

As the book of Job takes us through the continued struggles of his life, we start to understand his pain and frustration on a personal level. He wants to speak with God but often feels unheard, and he is continually battling over who to trust. Yet in the end, God shows up and does what only He can do. He has deep and personal conversations with Job, and it leads to God's restorative power in Job's life.

The entire book of Job is one of the most relatable depictions of trauma, anxiety, depression, and even worship in a cycle that seems to repeat itself. Job's cries to the Lord and expressions to those around him emphasize the pain he was facing:

> If only my anguish could be weighed
>> and all my misery be placed on the scales!
> It would surely outweigh the sand of the seas—
>> no wonder my words have been impetuous.
>
> Job 6:2–3

> And now my life ebbs away;
>> days of suffering grip me.

> Night pierces my bones;
>> my gnawing pains never rest.
>>> Job 30:16–17

In his pain and confusion, Job continues to speak highly of God's name, and expresses his desire to reason with God, acknowledging God's sovereignty and honor in his life (1:20–22, 13:3). And as the One who knows and sees all, the final word belongs to God, as He honors Job's diligence even through his despair.

> The Lord blessed the latter part of Job's life more than the former part. . . . Job lived a hundred and forty years; he saw his children and their children to the fourth generation.
>> Job 42:12, 16

God mends Job's heart throughout the entire journey. God fixes it all in the end.

It's likely that if we look into our own lives, we can see the results of God's grace, mercy, love, truth—and fixing. I know for me, one way I have seen the results of God's grace is in writing music. Many of my songs come out of difficult times and are born out of things I didn't know how God was going to fix.

"Not Alone" was written for a friend whose son was given only a few years left to live. I wanted her to understand that even in her pain, she did not have to face her battle alone. I hoped that she would press in to the hope and comfort that could only be found in Jesus, and that just like Job, she would have a moment with God in the end, knowing that He was there all along.

"Just a Friend" was written for every girl who is his "friend" when she wants to be more. When I sat down with my friend to write the verses, we kept getting distracted, excited about the hope we'd be sharing with every girl who listened to this song. We didn't want to give the

It's likely that if we look into our own lives, we can see the results of God's grace, mercy, love, truth—and fixing.

illusion that the song would fix everything or that she even *needed* to be fixed, but we wanted our melodies to create a safe place just in case she started to feel broken.

"Fix Things" was written from the same place. I wrote the first words, shared here, as I sat at my piano in my small hometown of Lithonia, Georgia, and wept, thinking about both Job and my mom. Even though my mom lives with an incurable chronic pain condition, she remains one of the most passionate and joyful people I know. Through the day-to-day of persistent physical discomfort, she chooses her faith, her family, her friends, and her life, when the easy choice would be to give up.

> *I know Your history*
> You are the One who sees
> And You fix things

These songs—these moments in life—remind me that I am not the one who is supposed to fix things. Sometimes I have the privilege and the opportunity to be a part of seeing something come to life that seemed to have lost its breath. But ultimately, the healing can only come from a place that is much greater than I am.

And even when God doesn't fix things how and when we want, He promises us heaven. He promises a place of no pain, hurting, or sickness—a place where everything is fixed. He promises a solution to every problem and freedom from every struggle.

I believe in heaven.

I believe in this perfect place.

I believe in the God who is *over* heaven—and earth.

So why do I try to take on the task of fixing everything instead? Why do I still struggle with giving up control and leaning in to the truth that *it's okay if I can't fix things.*

That is possibly my least favorite sentence that I have ever typed. While I know it is truth, my heart wants to believe that those italicized words *aren't* true. But it's okay if I can't fix things, and I will be okay with that.

FINDING QUIET

If you are a fixer like me, I hope this chapter serves as a reminder that you don't have to fix everything. But everything around you that *is* fixed is an example of the grace of the God who created us. His ability to fix the most thoroughly broken things can be the source of what holds our heads up in moments when we cannot find the cures we are looking for.

Even so, as fixers, we have a difficult time seeking rest when we see an opportunity to move, adjust—to fix. So in an effort to bring quiet into our lives, these are the things we will hold on to:

1. We are not alone.

You are not alone! While you may feel isolated at times, or even choose to isolate yourself, there are so many more people who are waiting to see what God is going to do in their lives, and He is holding in His hands every single cable to each of our hearts. Some things are going to take a really long time to figure out, yet in the process, your story could reach other people as you choose to share what God is doing, and in those moments, He will show you a community of others who need support just as you do.

2. "Just . . ."

- just a friend who wants to be more
- just an assistant when you desire be an executive
- just accepted into community college when you want to be attending an Ivy League university
- just coping with an illness instead of living fully without pain

The word *just* is synonymous with *simply* or *no more than*. In seasons of *just*, we are often wanting more, waiting on a solution, and we feel there is something in our lives that could be fixed that *just* isn't. But know that your current season is worth celebrating, regardless of what any other season could be. Embrace what you once called "just" as a "now," and know that now is a *good* thing. Trust that the season you are in is worth living in, even if it feels unfixable or unfinished.

3. Trust the One who fixes things.

God will fix it. You might not know how or when He will fix the things you have prayed over and wept for, but we *do* know that His timing for *all* things is *always* right, and whether on earth or in heaven, He *will* come through.

> Yes, my soul, find rest in God;
>> my hope comes from him.
> Truly he is my rock and my salvation;
>> he is my fortress, I will not be shaken.
>
> Psalm 62:5–6

four

I Am Not Enough

I will never be enough.

It seems anticlimactic to journey my way toward freedom with a seemingly negative acknowledgment. But truly, it's one of the first steps to letting go of the noise and stress of anxiety. A first step I have repeated many times . . . but a first step nonetheless.

I will never be enough.

I have spent a lot of my adult life finding joy when other people have already found it. Whether I've given advice, attention, money, or time, I thrive and grow on others' appreciation. Unfortunately, it's not always easy to know when the line should be drawn or when boundaries should be put up. For me, it's easy to not only be grateful to have been a part of their growth, but to want to be there for every step. And to feel guilty when I can't.

I will never be enough.

But there is One who is enough. Philippians 4:19 says, "And my God will meet all your needs according to the riches of his glory in Christ Jesus."

What if I could live like God will meet all needs and I don't have to?

Why is it so hard to do this?

Striving to Be Enough

I want to say this: Striving got "bad" for me when instant messaging became a thing. Remember the old-school online chat rooms? AOL Instant Messenger was practically my best friend. I woke up thinking about chatting with my friends, laughed as I reminisced on our conversations throughout the day, and often stayed up too late "talking" to them at night.

The word *instant* explains exactly how most of my peers operated and how I interpreted the need. *I have to get back to my friends* was a constant thought. I wanted to reply to messages instantly. If they said something funny, I wanted to let them know that it was hilarious—instantly. If they needed advice, prayer, encouragement, or support—I wanted to give an instant response.

Before this, I would catch up with friends the next time I saw them at school or youth group, but Instant Messenger and my obsession with it made everything an immediate need. There was no more waiting because everything was at my fingertips, every need quickly met. And I, the fixer and encourager and finder of joy in the joy of others, took this to heart.

Even though I battled a host of issues on my own and wasn't necessarily called "friend," I was still a pastor's kid who vocalized her desire to be like her parents—to be an encourager and a support system. I was only fourteen when it started to become a reality. I was making YouTube videos sharing my journey battling Tourette Syndrome, and playing live shows sharing songs and a message of hope and joy, even through my pain.

Within my peer group, and somewhat publicly, I was starting to become a go-to person for advice and support. Instant Messenger would only shine a brighter light on these unique relationships, but little did I know, it could get even more personal.

Sometime in the early 2000s there seemed to be a near explosion in the way we all communicated. There were brief moments of hype with sites like Friendster, Hi5, and the transition to chatting on Skype. I, like many other teens, fell in love with MySpace, which would later translate into a love for Facebook and Twitter, and my Sidekick cell phone would become my closest companion. Texting and social media became the main sources of communication between me and my friends, family, peers, and a new group I was learning about: *fans.*

The need for expedited responses grew as my phone was now in my pocket, with me everywhere. I coveted the ability of others who could say "I'm not available," because I hadn't yet reached that point. I felt the completely irrational and unhealthy need to be all things to all people at all times at whatever cost. I wanted to make sure everyone was not only okay, but also happy, filled with joy, and thriving. Even if it was at the expense of my own sanity.

I will never be enough.

Years later, at age twenty-eight, I daily remind myself that I will never be enough. I cannot be the sole giver of advice for a stranger, a peer, or even a friend. I cannot be readily available for the midnight call of everyone I love. I cannot be the hero. I cannot fix everything. I was not created to solve every problem or even listen to every detail of said problem's complexities. I am not enough. And that's okay. Because God is.

I am not enough. And that's okay. Because God is.

I want to acknowledge that the preceding paragraph is an example of me speaking truth to my anxiety. With every word I typed, I was overwhelmed with guilt and shame that I can't save the day. I have no interest in parading around as though I'm a hero, yet imagining a world where I'm not supposed to try to be one makes me feel as though I'm not doing enough.

When someone texts me, I want to respond right away, but I'm immediately held back. I sometimes feel as though I'm going through stages of grief. And guilt. And shame.

Stage 1: I worry about my ability to keep up the conversation. I don't know the other person's expectations or intentions, so I worry that I won't be able to meet their standards.

Stage 2: Now I'm thinking about intentions. I begin to get frustrated, remembering the times I thought I was having a casual conversation and it turned out that someone wanted a video for their cousin who is a big fan, or they wanted me to swing by their church and "sing a little" that Wednesday night. I don't know what people want, or whether it's fair for me to question it, so how can I know if I should reply?

Stage 3: I feel guilty for doubting their intentions. There are *so* many incredible people I have met who have the purest heart and would never try to manipulate our relationship. *What if they're simply checking in on me or genuinely just want to say hi?* Well, now I feel like a jerk.

Stage 4: Everyone probably thinks I'm a jerk. They probably think that I "got famous" and forgot about them, and they sit around and exchange texts about how I'm not the same. And if they don't say it, they certainly think it. The way that I've felt betrayed by others is the same way they feel now. I've let them down, and even if I reply to this text, the reality is that I'll keep letting everyone down.

Stage 5: This stage resembles Stage 1, where I'm unaware of what the expectations are. So often I'll get a text that starts off with, "I know you're busy, so no pressure, but . . ." and that *should* relieve pressure. But what if they're just saying that? What if it means that no one really gets enough from me, so everyone has come to expect less of me? *You haven't tried hard enough. You haven't given enough. You're not enough. So don't even try.*

Fifty-plus unread text messages later:

Why even try?

In these low moments, I have to remind myself: *It's not just me.* I was becoming a teenager when the internet was getting more popular than ever. More and more people had devices they carried around with them at all times, and as technology advanced, so did our need to embrace it every minute of every day.

It's practically unheard of for someone under thirty to take more than a few hours to respond to a text. And if they do, they should be prepared with a reason why or it could cause friction in relationships. This amount of expectancy weighs on me as I hear the ding of my phone while I'm with my family, reading a book, writing a song, or if I simply don't feel like being on my phone. I'm not old enough for anyone to believe I'm not on my phone all day.

As a mom, the only logical answer that will get me off the hook is that my daughter is resting or fussing or needs my attention. But what if that's not the reason I don't respond right away? As much as it challenges me, a people pleaser, to admit it, sometimes people aren't at the top of my list. Sometimes rest or hobbies are—or simply quiet time. But alas, it's nearly impossible to convey that in a way that doesn't cause complexities with the person who sends the text.

When I was in elementary school, if I wanted to talk with friends about a band that I loved, I had to wait until I saw them in school and hope they had heard the same new song I did. But by the time I was in middle school, I had a laptop with internet access, on which I could talk instantly through forums and group chats. As time went on, technology improved, and the opportunities have become endless. But now, the anxiety and pressure of not being enough seem endless too.

When it comes to an email or text message, there is no end. Instagram feed? Endless. YouTube videos you could watch? Music you could listen to? Both endless—you don't even have to worry about how many gigs are on your iPod anymore. Contact list? Bottomless. No more physical address books that you could fill out and fill up. There is never enough time to go through it all. In this kind of world, no one can ever feel like they are enough.

Back in the day, artists could release new songs or a full-length album and go out on tour, and immediately after resume their regular lives. Now there's the pressure to be "on" all the time—not just when you're at events or hanging out with people. When you're sitting at home, you're expected to create social media posts and casual "stories" to share the ins and outs of every day so people feel involved in your life.

I'm grateful that I enjoy social media, because it doesn't feel like a chore. But there are still moments when I wonder, *What would it be like to do this only because I love it and not because the expectation is continuously, increasingly rooted in the value of the instantaneous?*

A Break from Enough

In 2017, Morgan and I got to experience this firsthand. We filmed a genealogy-based reality-show challenge that follows four family teams of two across the country competing for $50,000 and meeting newfound family members along the way. We took DNA tests and traveled coast to coast, meeting extended family members we never knew we had!

One of the most compelling parts of the show is that you compete with no help from technology. We filmed for about ten days without the use of computers, GPS systems, or even the radio in the car. We used paper maps, our gut instincts, and a flip phone to complete some of the challenges throughout the adventure.

To make things even more interesting, we were not permitted to have communication with anyone outside of the show for the duration of the race. No friends, no family members back home—Morgan couldn't even update her husband on how we were doing! We were all-in with the race, and we hoped that somehow we'd bring home a win.

(Spoiler alert: We did not. We're terrible at sports and failed at most of the physical challenges. But we had a ton of fun, created a lot of memories—and went home in last place.)

Almost a year before filming the show, my music team and I planned the release of my third full-length—and first independent—album. We knew we would call it *'91* after the year I was born, and a little tribute to one of my favorite songs from an earlier album, *1945*. As most music is released on Fridays, I was excited to see that September 1—9.1—would land on a Friday, so it only made sense to release on that date.

Fast-forward to a year later: The reality show sent us the itinerary (or at least what could be shared without compromising its integrity and secrecy), and indicated they would be filming the last week of August and the first week of September.

The bottom line: I would be somewhere in the United States without a phone or access to the internet on the day the album would be released.

It's never great for an artist to be out-of-pocket for nearly two weeks—and on Release Day of all days?! There were interviews to have and social media updates to make! My publicist and manager were supportive yet nervous, as it was a risk to the album's success for me to unplug at this magnitude. Consequently, we had many conversations about changing the release date (but why release an album called *'91* on 9.8?) or even what would happen if I couldn't film the show. But ultimately, it was my decision.

Let's do it.

The next ten-ish days were some of the most exhausting, exciting, and exhilarating days of our lives. Filming the show took every ounce of our emotional and physical energy in ways that are impossible to explain. Morgan and I followed clues and competed in challenges, each night leading us to the door of a distant cousin who would be our host for the evening; then we would wake up before sunrise and do it all over again.

As an artist whose job is to make noise, it was the quietest moment of my career—and it was simultaneously the most freeing.

On September 1, we woke up at our relative's house in Birmingham, Alabama, and got the clue that we would be driving to and meeting family in our hometown of Atlanta, Georgia. So many emotions filled my head as we hopped in the car and started our drive. We were completely focused on the race, but in a moment of quiet, Morgan asked me, "How do you feel?"

It was my album release day, and unlike every other release day for the last eight years, there were no early morning radio interviews or email-based magazine interviews. I wasn't retweeting positive reactions or commenting on Instagram posts about the record. I didn't know which of my friends were streaming my new songs, and had no idea what my fans were thinking.

As an artist whose job is to make noise, it was the quietest moment of my career—and it was simultaneously the most freeing.

For the first time in my entire career, I genuinely experienced what it felt like to share something you believe in without worrying what other people will think.

My ultimate goal in creating music is to inspire and encourage everyone who listens, but before it reaches other people, I have to feel confident about what I am creating. So while I did feel a little anxious not knowing if the songs were reaching people in a positive way, the absence of *any* response allowed me to ask myself how *I* genuinely felt about what I was creating.

Sometimes my goal while creating can become overshadowed by the pressure to be *enough*. When writing songs and choosing what goes on each project, I get overwhelmed because I want to make sure the college freshman listening to it finds it relatable and feels compelled to share it not only with her friends, but also with her younger sister, her brother-in-law, parents, and colleagues. I want to write specifically for people and their stories but can easily feel like I'm not doing enough if every single person who listens doesn't hear something that reaches them.

I should note that I'm not particularly concerned with how people perceive my voice or talent. I am fully aware that it's unrealistic for every listener to become a fan. I'm not offended if people don't vibe with my style or have an overwhelming reaction to how I sing or play the guitar. I just want everyone who hears my words to know that they are seen and known.

But I will never be enough for everyone.

In my efforts to create, share, and make others feel all of the in-depth feels, I have to continually remind myself that I was not created to be *enough*. I know that I was not created to be *the source* of hope, joy, or love. So I have to consciously, while I am creating, make choices that direct to the ultimate Source. And when I release music and am told by a reviewer, new listener, or lifelong fan that my words have left a lasting impression, I acknowledge that I'm merely a vessel sharing a message from the One who *is* enough.

Releasing an album with absolutely no contact with the outside world was one of the greatest decisions I could ever make. I set out a goal to create songs that I loved, and maybe even bless someone in the process. I sent those songs into the world *without* the need to scroll and refresh to receive instant gratification—or instant negativity that would cause me to become anxious and ready to isolate or clap back.

On our last day of filming (also known as the morning after we lost the competition), we went to the airport and got ready to check in for our recently booked flight home. Just before we said our official good-byes to the production team, they handed us our smartphones. While it wasn't even two weeks without it, it felt foreign to hold it, and though I turned it on, I didn't look at the screen until moments later.

When I did, I was overwhelmed. In the best way. I saw texts, social media notifications, and missed calls from my team, fans, family, and friends. There were so many encouraging messages about the album, and I even found out that it charted at number one in its category on iTunes. I was beaming from ear to ear, overjoyed to receive so much love on a project that meant so much to me. But truthfully, after just a few minutes of swiping and scrolling, I put my phone away.

All the pressure to share my instant reactions and immediate responses came flooding in. And the second I closed my phone, and it was *quiet*, the pressure went away.

That week was the first time I realized how much I needed to implement boundaries when it came to my phone. I've had times in the past where I'd check my email only on certain days, or I'd turn my phone off by a certain time at night, but a two-week separation from my phone followed by an instant flood of communication was the wake-up call I needed to embrace the quiet.

As much as I love social media, chatting with friends, and technology as a whole, there's something beautiful about embracing *quiet.* Nothing can replace eradicating the itch . . . the need . . . the near *compulsion* to read, respond, and repeat. There's a freedom that comes along with not feeling like you *have* to scroll so you don't miss out on what's new, and you *must* post so no one forgets you exist.

So I started to leave my phone charger (including the portable one) in my room, office, and car—exclusively.

It may seem crazy to some and it certainly may not work for all, but not allowing my phone charger in the common areas of my home where I spend time with family and friends often means one of two things will happen:

1. My phone will die and my only option is to be present with those around me.
2. My phone will start to die and I have to put it in another room to charge—so my only option is to be present with those around me.

This small change made a significant difference in my life. I *love* socializing and being present, so taking away the ability to use my phone was far from something I *had* to do. But removing my phone directly from my hand throughout the day encouraged more natural conversation with my friends and family. And when I needed to reply to someone, or thought of a post I could make, *then* I would grab my phone. I was no longer constantly scrolling through places I *could* be, people I *could* be talking to, and things I *could* be posting.

I later added another change: Instead of the traditional charging cable, I implemented a charging dock that sits on my nightstand and charges my phone. This eliminates the capabilities for me to lie in my bed scrolling or swiping through posts, apps, and games, finding a false sense of peace and quiet through technology that was only adding more pressure. Now I have no choice but to dock my phone on the nightstand while it charges. It may have started off as a *need* because there was no other way my phone could charge, but it has gradually become something I *want* to do after seeing how much more easily I fall asleep at night, and how much genuine peace I receive from going to bed with a clear mind.

Setting boundaries in my everyday life with my phone, social media, and other areas of communication, especially via technology, has allowed me to embrace the concept that not only am I not enough, but I don't *have* to be. Stepping away and realizing that lives are still being lived, advice is still being given, and everyone and everything is still okay *without me*, reminds me that it is not my job to be enough.

We Are Not Enough

I remember replying to a text one day about a work request. I don't remember exactly what the sender's text was, or what mine was for that matter, but I know that it was related to a song or a tour—and I had received it *months* prior. I had a lot going on at the time and, as you now know, I constantly deal with the stress of *how*, *when*, *if*, and *why* when it comes to conversations.

When I finally responded, he took a screenshot and posted it to his Instagram story, making a joke about how long it had taken me to text him back.

I believe I messaged him, making a joke about it. And I may have even reposted it. All out of desperation to validate his feelings, and to eradicate any glimpse that I might have any. But truthfully?

I felt small.

I felt embarrassed.

I felt like I let him down.

I felt like I let everyone down.

I felt that the reason I hadn't texted back was completely valid, but all of a sudden that didn't matter because someone else was affected by my inability to be enough for them. I had chosen my own rest, emotions, and time over his, to prioritize moments in my life over messages.

I felt that I was not enough.

And the best part is—I was not. I am not. And I never will be.

What if we lived in a world where we didn't expect people to give of themselves when we ask?

What if we lived our lives without the presumption that just because we ask or request, we should receive?

What if we didn't have the anticipation that our wants are near demands and must be met within a certain time frame?

Now, let's be clear: This isn't applicable to a boss assigning a task to an employee or a parent directing a child to complete their chores. We're not talking about a husband and wife finding compromise or a teacher setting the precedent for how her classroom operates.

This is about the war of instantaneousness taking over our peace of mind. This directly relates to pressure we put on our friends, followers, and dare I say, fans to validate our thoughts, feelings, and wants.

What if we operated in a way that *didn't* add that pressure?

What if we loved a swift text back but didn't make someone feel guilty for not providing it?

What if we got excited over new likes and follows but didn't question our worth without them?

> *What if we embraced the moments when He uses us to extend His grace, mercy, and love to others—yet allowed Him to do the work?*

What if we were thrilled about a reply after a DM says Seen, but we knew that without one, our value hasn't changed? Maybe they're busy, overwhelmed, or forgetful.

What if we removed the pressure that most of us face and instead added peace and quiet to the lives of the ones we love?

Remember Philippians 4:19: "And my God will meet all your needs according to the riches of his glory in Christ Jesus."

What if we acted like those words were true?

What if we acted like God will meet all needs and we don't have to?

What if we embraced the moments when He uses us to extend His grace, mercy, and love to others—yet allowed Him to do the work?

What if we stopped asking *What if*... and we jumped right in?
I want to.
And I want you to join me.

FINDING QUIET

Together we can celebrate the quiet that comes without the noise, the advice, the fixing, and the phones, knowing that we don't have to be enough for anyone. Knowing that the joy, peace, and stability of others is not contingent on our presence and that rest will only come when we welcome it.

Together we will welcome the ease that comes with letting go of what we don't have to hold. And as we find this peace for ourselves, we will return the favor to others.

We will choose not to add pressure to people. While we may love a swift text back, we won't make anyone feel guilty for not providing it, and even if we get excited over new likes and follows, or a DM that says Seen, their presence or absence doesn't change our value.

We will invest in our needs being met by the One who is enough for everyone and all things. And we will step back from the instant and immediate, allowing Him to do His best work.

When you start to feel like the only solution to finding quiet is becoming the solution to everyone's needs, remember:

1. You will not be enough—and that's okay.
2. You have direct access to God—*the* Source—who was, is, and will forever be enough for you.

3. We not only get to enjoy the privilege of connection that we have with the Source, but we get to share in that joy with others. We can direct people to the Word of God and the promises of God, instead of attempting to take on the responsibility to remedy everything on our own.

five

Learning to Let Go

"Don't move, I'll be right back," I jokingly, and regularly, tell my daughter. It's a joke because she's an infant. And when she's safely lying in her bassinet while I run to grab a toy or her bottle, there isn't much moving that she can do. I know it's a lame joke, but I always get a good laugh because that's what moms do. We get good little laughs to ourselves about the most random, everyday things. (Full disclosure: I've always laughed at my incredibly lame jokes even before I had a baby.)

Truthfully, if Isabella *could* move, it would be a different story. And maybe my instructions now are a kind of practice for later. There will come a time when she's crawling, then walking, and even running. I'll say "Don't move" to her, expecting that she'll oblige. Ultimately, she's human and will make her own choices, so for those moments that I am away, I am letting go of my control.

My sister told me to start practicing that muscle—the letting-go-of-control muscle. Our kids are only eight days apart (Crazy! Exciting! Not planned!—now back to the book), and they spend a lot of time with our parents, affectionately known as G-pop and Goldie. On a family vacation to Florida, my sister and I headed out to lunch with our husbands and planned to leave the kids with the grandparents. I fully trust my parents' capabilities to raise and parent children. Not only am I grateful for my own childhood, but I have seen them foster and assist in co-parenting a significant number of children in our local community. I have little to no doubts and very minimal fear, but there's nothing like the unexpected anxiety of leaving your kid in someone else's care.

As we were leaving, I felt myself getting anxious, going over the checklist with my mom to make sure they had the bottles and gripe water and diapers. I was firing questions all while giving them the answers and double-checking everything with my husband along the way. I was the last one of the four of us to get in the car, and we were only five minutes into the car ride when I told my sister, "I need to spend more time around you."

That wasn't an odd revelation. Anyone who knows me knows that my sister is my oldest friend and confidant. I will ask her advice on life, business, and friendship for hours on end and tell you all about her latest creative projects. Like now, I am currently deviating from my book to tell you all about how I like to tell people all about her.

"I need to know how you are so calm when it's time to let go," I continued.

Morgan took a minute, and in a moment of attempting to simply speak her mind, she completely shifted my own.

She told me that someday Jacob, her son, would grow up. He would go over to friends' houses and want to go out with them to concerts, maybe even take a road trip with them when he's older. He would someday move out and maybe even start a family of his own. Morgan emphasized that she (with Patrick, her husband) was raising Jacob to be equipped for all of those things, and those would all be moments when she would have to let go.

"I know I'll have to let go in bigger ways in the future, so I choose to find peace in the smaller moments right now," she said. "I'm practicing using the muscle of letting go."

It reminded me of a film I watched years ago. The main character, Grace, is a high school graduate who moves across the country to purse her dreams of becoming a singer-songwriter. She battles in her relationship with God and in her relationship with her parents, who would have preferred that she stay closer to home and not pursue a career that was seemingly all about *fame.* Back home, she was a worship leader alongside her dad at the local church, but her newfound passion seems to be taking her down the wrong path.

After she left home, there's a scene where her dad and their pastor are talking. Her dad is expressing his worry and fear about his daughter being negatively influenced by her surroundings and getting involved with people who don't have her best interest at heart.

The pastor simply replies, "God may not be using you in Grace's life right now . . . or He may never. But He *is* in control."

That scene has become my go-to recollection when I'm thinking about the muscle of letting go. It may seem a bit ironic because I *am* a touring artist, but the message of this film isn't about a career choice or even a geographic location. The heart of the story is learning to let go even when we *think* we know what's best—and even when we *do* know what's best.

I should probably offer full disclosure that it's possible I am in this film, *Grace Unplugged*. I play Rachel, the best friend of Grace. While I read the script prior to my audition, I wasn't on set for this particular scene and didn't see it until the film had been shot and edited. Of all the fun scenes with music, and even through all the giddiness I felt at acting alongside AJ Michalka (Grace), this scene continues to be my favorite.

Jeremiah 29:11 is one of the most popular Bible verses. This is already my second time referencing it in this book alone. You can often count on youth pastors using it in at least two sermons a year, and you can find it printed on shirts, posters, and books all over the world—and for good reason! It's an incredible verse: "'For I know the plans I have for you,' declares the LORD, 'plans to prosper you and not to harm you, plans to give you hope and a future.'"

I read those words and I know that whatever my future, I am going to be okay because God's got my back. He will remain in control as He has been all this time, so I don't have to worry. Yet as a parent, I have to remind myself that this Scripture doesn't apply exclusively to me. It is applicable to everyone, and that includes my daughter, Isabella. So in moments when I'm apprehensive about losing an ounce of control, I have to allow Jeremiah 29:11 to remind me that God knows the plans He has for me—and my daughter—and He will forever follow through on the promise of hope.

Those were the words that the fictional yet wise pastor in the film was speaking. He wanted to emphasize that God hadn't removed His plan from Grace's or her dad's lives; it was simply possible that God wasn't going to use her dad in that moment.

I genuinely enjoy allowing Jeremiah 29:11 to speak into my life when it comes to my health. I face challenging days more often than I'd prefer, but I know that whether on earth or in heaven, God will heal me as a part of His plan. I have faith in who He is, and that is what allows me to move forward.

But what about my career? Am I letting go in seasons when I'm not as busy as seasons past? Or am I wanting to have complete control as I'm waiting for an important phone call and putting my hope in hearing a yes?

And what about in my friendships and relationships? Am I inviting unnecessary anxiousness by worrying when I don't need to? Am I embracing the people God has put in my life, or am I trying to do everything myself?

Knowing the plans God has for us is an action. It's one thing to hear something in school or in a work meeting, but when you actually study it, you *know* it, and soon it's a part of how you live and breathe. I want to do better at *knowing* that God has plans for me, whether I know these plans or not. And I want to put that knowledge into action and continue to exercise the muscle of letting go.

I want to do better at <u>knowing</u> that God has plans for me . . . to put that knowledge into action and continue to exercise the muscle of letting go.

I don't like working that muscle. If I'm honest, I don't really like working any muscles. When it comes to physical fitness, you can tell your muscles are developing and growing when you've targeted them with strength and resistance pressure and they start to feel that increasing muscle burn. When *I* go to the gym, I like to try something new every time so I don't feel that pressure. Occasionally I enjoy the push and pull that comes with a good workout, but ultimately, if I start to hurt, I want to stay home the next day.

Whether we choose to work our physical muscles at the gym or not, we have no choice when it comes to exercising the muscle of letting go. We *can* choose to run and operate every aspect of our lives, and even try to control the details of the lives of those around us, but ultimately that will crash and burn. We were not made to survive and thrive completely on our own, and the sooner we learn not only to ask for help, but to embrace our communities in *their* strengths, the better off we'll be.

I want to have freedom in the peace that comes with letting go, but I have a difficult time putting in the work.

I want to celebrate the joy of letting go in the major moments, but the smaller ones consume my energy and time.

I've wrestled most of my life with nervousness and fears. I've worked hard to get past *most* of my fears, but some things still make me feel a bit uneasy. Like many people, I'm not thrilled with heights or things that are suspended.

Nonetheless, I love zip-lining.

I don't know how I have come to love something that also terrifies me, but it is what it is. I even hate the climbing-up part. I feel my legs simultaneously tensing up while they're shakier than they've ever been. And my arms feel like they are on fire while my mind is trying to convince myself that it's a good idea. Every inch I get higher up the ladder, the thought of *What am I doing?* increases in intensity, yet I keep going, because I'm going to love the feeling on the way down. Or across. You know, as you go.

The first time I was on a zip line I was only about six years old. I was in a gymnastics program at an incredible gym. I had just seen Dominique Moceanu compete in the Olympics, and I was inspired to become a gymnast, so my gracious parents enrolled me in classes.

The zip line was nearly the entire length of the gym. There were blocks to climb (no ladder, thankfully), and at the very end, where you would let go, was the infamous pit. It was six to eight feet deep of fluffy yet firm foam. I later learned that it was incredibly common for gymnastics centers to have a pit, but honestly I thought that we were the coolest of the cool. I had seen some zip lines on TV that ended on the ground or simply at a platform that looked like the starting one, but a pit?! Winning!

Unlike the zip line at a summer camp or theme park, our gym simply had the line that was connected to a handle bar, and no harnesses or helmets—you simply grabbed on to the handlebars, put your feet in the air, and went zooming (er, zipping) across the gym.

There are two moments in this process when you have to let go.

First, when you dismount the blocks to start soaring down the line. You're not letting go with your hands, so it may seem like it isn't "letting go," but without that physical action of leaving the blocks, you'll never leave your starting point. You have to choose to gently push off from the blocks, put your feet in the air, and let gravity do its job. You have to choose to let go.

I still have vivid memories of the first time I let go. I was afraid because I had never seen a zip line in person, and I had certainly never been on one. But I knew that all the other girls were watching me and that my coach was depending on me, so in an effort to make everyone proud and not hold up the line, I did it.

I squeezed my eyes shut and held my breath, and *I let go.*

Then I was zipping across the gym. I opened my eyes and allowed myself to take in everything around me. My breathing sped up as my heart rate increased, and my body felt a rush of excitement and freedom as I felt the wind in my hair. It seemed the room was slowing down around me as I flew past everyone doing slow-motion uneven bars and floor routines.

I found myself smiling bigger than I had in a *long* time.

It was a smile that *screamed* joy. **Pure joy.** And I fell in love with the freeing result of letting go.

Then:

"Let go!"

My coach screamed for me to let go as I got closer to the end of the zip line. I needed to let go, as I would soon be right above the pit, and if I *didn't*, the abrupt ending of the zip line would jolt me down instead. (I found this out from experience later on.)

I let go.

And I landed in the pile of foam—the pit.

While the foam was a bit itchy and had an odd smell of gym and cleaning supplies, I remember feeling safe. I felt secure and comforted in the big, practical, and somehow even comical pit of foam.

I didn't have much time before I had to crawl out of the pit as another girl geared up to take her turn. The actual moment of being on the zip line felt like a lifetime, but it was less than fifteen seconds in its entirety. But sometimes you don't need an extended period of a beautiful thing. Simply a glimpse can be enough.

When I first let go from the block platform, I flew through the gym, experiencing such a reckless abandon that nothing but speed and freedom seemed to matter. And by simply letting go from *that*, I felt security and assurance that gave me a peace and a sense of safety. Letting go can feel like an intimidating and uneasy choice. But the result is always something worth experiencing.

I would have another gymnastics-related lesson in letting go later on, but it wasn't one that I wanted to learn.

Losing Control and Learning to Let Go

Shortly after this zip line experience, my symptoms of Tourette Syndrome started showing up. The tics were a challenge at home, but I was able to fight through it for those first few months. And even though it was difficult and often times embarrassing while I was out in public, I remember having hope in the early stages of my tics that maybe they would just go away.

But they didn't.

And pursuing gymnastics became one of my greatest obstacles.

I remember one specific occasion on the balance beam. My coach, who was walking beside me on the floor to make sure I didn't lose my balance, was telling me to *pivot* while keeping my legs steady and my arms stretched out.

I couldn't do it.

She continued to give me instruction, but my tics were getting in the way. Little did I know, nervousness increased the severity, so not being able to complete the simple tasks she gave me only made my tics worse.

I tried to keep my legs where they were supposed to be, but they kept moving and I kept losing my balance.

I tried to keep my arms straight out, but I couldn't keep them from bending inward.

I tried to stay focused, but I kept squeezing my eyes shut and throwing my head down.

It was a disaster.

The situation escalated from an inability to do what my coach asked into a seemingly defiant child deliberately making everything worse. My coach was getting frustrated, and I heard the sternness in her voice, but I couldn't even find the words to tell her that I couldn't help it. Because who would believe me?

Before I knew it, my leg twitched so bad that it hit my coach. "Ugh!" She expressed pain from the aggressive kick. She backed away from the balance beam with her hand over her face, and every ounce of my confidence and joy was gone.

That was my last day in gymnastics. I grew up with a million dreams of all the things I wanted to do and all the careers I wanted to embark upon, but gymnastics was always at the top of the list. Even though my parents could barely afford it, they knew how badly I wanted to be a gymnast and maybe even pursue the Olympics, so they made a way. But because of the severity of my tics, that was a dream that I had to give up.

I had to let go.

It's not as freeing or fun to let go of something you want to keep holding on to, and as time went on, I realized that I was having to continually exercise that muscle of letting go. I had to remind myself that the season of participating in gymnastics, while amazing, had come to an end. I had to choose to accept that the dream I had of being a professional gymnast was *not* going to be accomplished. I had to accept that it was time to let go.

That experience taught me how to truly grieve a dream that simply wouldn't come true. Some may say to never give up on those dreams and to always work hard to make them happen, but looking back, I know that letting go was the best decision for me. Because without that dream falling apart, I would have never spent that spare time alone at home. And while that may sound sad, those moments of alone time turned into moments of creating and dreaming new dreams. In those moments, I wrote songs and screenplays and discovered that my love for singing was more than something I desired to do locally.

Letting go of one of my biggest dreams ended up leading me to an even bigger one.

Letting go of one of my biggest dreams ended up leading me to an even bigger one. And while I have moments when I look back and wish I had learned how to do a back handspring, I couldn't be more grateful as I think about the life that I am blessed to live.

FINDING QUIET

Are you learning to let go?

Maybe you're learning to let go of a dream that may not come true. Or maybe you're letting go of a friendship or relationship that wasn't what you thought it would be. Maybe you're learning to let go of something someone said that hurt you, or something *you* said that's already been forgiven. Or maybe you're like me, learning to let go as your child grows and is learning to be more independent.

I want to leave you with three steps you can take today toward letting go and finding peace. They may seem like small steps, but know that every step you make is one step closer to embracing trust, and whether a big or small step, it's still worth taking.

1. **Embrace the quiet.** Set a timer for five minutes and embrace a quiet moment when you do not go back to the very thing you are choosing to let go. Allow your mind to be filled with things that bring you peace instead of things that could be a burden.

2. **Journal.** Imagine what it would be like to fully trust that you are capable of letting go, and journal what you come up with. What would it mean to let go? What would it mean to feel freedom? What would it mean to feel safe?

3. **Tell a friend and listen to their response.** Tell a trustworthy and encouraging friend that you are struggling with letting go, and ask them what they would do in your situation. You don't have to take notes and follow

their advice word for word, but by welcoming someone else into your corner, you are accepting that you can't face this alone, and by sharing your experience with them, you literally are letting go of it.

Hope. 11.15.19.

In.

Out.

Two words used to explain the two options for going through a door.

In.

And Out.

The phrase my parents used throughout my childhood to explain how long we would be in the grocery store. And we were sometimes in there a little longer than

In. And out.

The description used by my surgeon that was to represent the simple explanation of my nasal surgery. A quick outpatient procedure and I should stop having chronic sinus issues.

In.

Out.

The simplest rules that create a pattern to continue sending and receiving air through our lungs.

And just like my surgery it's much more complex but to use two simple words explains it the best—the breath goes in as we take it all in and the breath goes out as we send it out.

And just like my parents when they would take us to run errands, going through different aisles to get all we need before going to the checkout lane there is much more that happens in between the in and the out as our organs play a melody the choir can't live without. But all we see is the simplistic remix, the in and out. The beginning and end.

Breath.

We take a breath.

Most of us take for granted how easy it is for to us take a breath.

As a kid who battled asthma and an adult who still carries an inhaler I oftentimes have to take conscious breaths.

In.

Out.

I remind myself to take the steps. The simple steps. Even on the days where it feels like I can't.

On the days when work isn't fun anymore.
To love what you do and never work a day?
But what about the days where I'm working and I love it but it's still a pain.

And on the days when my family is far from perfect.
The days when apologies and insecurities are colliding and colluding and I feel so insecure I start to wonder if it was all worth it.

And on the days when the news makes me angry.
Where change seems unrealistic and middle ground seems like an impossible dream.

On the days when my car seems like it won't start.
When I try to make breakfast but everything ends up burned.
When I'm an hour from home and my phone is on 1%.

*When I start to doubt the choice to live on the West Coast
and pay this much in rent.*

*On the days when I'm tired of shopping but I still haven't
found what I'm looking for.*

*You too have had these moments when you're just hoping
for an open door.*

*When my health is failing me
Friends aren't around.
When my confidence is too quiet
When my fears are too loud.*

*When everything is just as it seems, broken pictures and
scattered dreams and everything I want is confused
with what I need but it doesn't even matter because
none of it is coming to me.*

*When I feel alone.
When I am alone.*

Somehow.

There is still hope.

*Because just like the motions it takes to go through a
door, my body is ready to do the only consistent thing
that life brings forth.
In.
Out.
It tells me that there is still a chance to recover.
In.
Out.
It tells me that right now won't last forever.
In.
Out.*

With each passing breath there is more promise of the next.
In.
Out.
In.
Out.

Sometimes soft.
Sometimes consistent.
Sometimes heavy.
Sometimes burdened.

Sometimes the in is because of surprise.
Sometimes the out is the reality of demise.

Sometimes the in is filled with disbelief.
Sometimes the out is the only form of relief.

In.
Out.

I will not take it for granted.
I will not lose sight of the only thing I know.
Because in a world of uncertainties and things I'm unsure
     of,
I will always remember that where there is breath—

there is hope.

six

The Desire for Control

I never liked the phrase *control freak*. I understand that it's meant to be a negative term for people who are obsessed with control, but as someone who loves schedules, planning, and organization, I was always confused.

How could wanting to have control be a bad thing?

I fully understand that obsessively controlling things or at least obsessively *wanting* to control things is definitely a damaging concept. When we start trying to control the lives of everyone around us or we fall apart when the decisions of other people affect our plans, we've definitely jumped into territory that is both unhealthy and unnecessary. But in order for my day-to-day life to seem somewhat structured, I *need* to have control.

And honestly, it's quite easy for me to pinpoint exactly when I started becoming fascinated with trying to regain and maintain control.

I was eleven years old when my diagnoses of Tourette Syndrome, OCD, ADHD, and anxiety were confirmed. But before I started having a lot of the symptoms that I still have now, even my birth was nothing shy of a miracle, as my parents tell the story. During my mom's pregnancy, as she was merely weeks away from her due date, the doctors couldn't find me on the ultrasound. The doctors talked to my dad, saying that it's possible my mom could have been making it up, as there was no way there was a baby. My parents went home and prayed, day after day, and at their next appointment, I was there. The medical staff was confused and blown away . . . but my parents weren't. They knew that they had witnessed what only God's grace could do, and that's how I got my middle name. But even once I was born, I still faced health challenges: For starters, I was hospitalized for pneumonia seven times before I was two years old. From there, I had persistent digestive issues.

Sometimes I worry about how my memories from the hospital often seem more vivid than the ones from home. And now, since I know so much about hospitalization, when one of my family members isn't feeling well, they'll likely call me for advice. And more often than not, if they call the doctor afterward, they'll hear very similar things.

My health complications became especially taxing when I was about nine and the symptoms of Tourette Syndrome started to show up.

Tourette Syndrome is a neurobiological condition causing involuntary movements and sounds, called tics. My tics started with my arms and legs. My arms would bend at a rapid pace, causing my balled-up fist to hit my shoulder. While standing, my legs would make similar movements, causing my foot to swiftly kick my rear. I also had a tic causing me to blink aggressively. What started as a normal blink would quickly turn into my eyes squeezing shut for sometimes close to ten seconds at a time. This would happen every thirty to forty seconds.

And the last of my initial tics was with my neck, as my head would bend downward and my chin would hit my chest. And verbally, I had a host of squeaking and squealing noises as well as phrases that I repeated over and over.

I learned early on about something called suppression. No one taught it to me; it seemed to come naturally, and I would later find out that it is one of the worst things someone with Tourette Syndrome can do. There's a phrase in the Tourette Syndrome community, "ticcing away," and when you suppress your tics—hold them back—they eventually catch up with you and display much worse than normal.

I started suppressing my tics when I was around other kids or just out in public. I was tired of people staring at me, and even laughing, pointing, and mocking. I figured that the only way to gain their approval was to force myself to no longer have my tics. Before I knew they were called tics, before I had even gotten a diagnosis, my family and I called them "jerks," because my body was jerking. We all knew that I was not in control over the jerks and jolts, but to me, the only thing worse than losing control was being completely ridiculed and isolated because of it.

So instead of allowing my tics to have a negative impact on my life, I spent hours at a time learning to control them. Sometimes people are impressed that I was able to suppress or "control" my tics, but in reality, when you're dealing with this neurological condition, the last thing you should do is suppress it, because it will catch up to you.

After spending time around other kids or running errands with my mom, I would be in so much pain from the suppression that when I got home, I would lie in my bed for hours at a time, my body ticcing so aggressively it wasn't safe for me to be anywhere else. My parents would take turns sitting with me and holding me as I cried and dealt with the realities of my life. They didn't want me to force myself to suppress in public, but I didn't want to be ridiculed everywhere we went. To me, the pain was the price paid for trying to have somewhat of a normal childhood.

Looking for Relief

I wish I could say that my diagnosis brought about a cure or even a medication that helped and that I lived happily ever after. But at age eleven, in the doctor's office and finding out that I have Tourette Syndrome (and OCD, ADHD, and anxiety), I was told that there was absolutely no cure for anything that I was facing. There were medications that might help, but ultimately, no one could tell me when, or if, it would ever get better.

I started medication soon after being diagnosed. My tics had become so physically harmful, we knew we had to try something. The only frustrating thing was that we would soon find out that the side effects of the medication were almost worse than the tics themselves. I started battling suicidal thoughts and losing sleep, and I had to be put on a heart monitor because one of the medications was affecting my organs. We would even take weekly, sometimes daily, trips to the fire station to get my blood pressure or oxygen levels checked, and sometimes I would go to the emergency room due to the results.

From ages eleven to fifteen I was on and off various medications, all in an effort to regain control of my own body. I entered a season when I stopped singing and stopped dancing around the house and making random videos to make my family laugh. I was a completely different kid. My sleep was disrupted, my mood was destroyed, and my personality deteriorated. And one of the medications was the start to a long battle with binge eating.

> *From ages eleven to fifteen I was on and off various medications, all in an effort to regain control of my own body.*

The next medication we tried would be the last. It was supposed to be "the one," the absolute source of hope. Yet it completely let me down.

I stopped participating in daily activities, such as playing outside, reading books, and even academics. There was a point when I literally stopped doing any kind of schoolwork. You would think that because I was homeschooled, my mom could work something out for me, but that wasn't even possible. I would just lie in bed for hours, staring at the wall, completely incapable of moving, because at that time, the only medication that would keep me safe caused me to completely shut down both physically and mentally.

And it simply wasn't worth it.

At fifteen years old, I was just one year away from going to college. One of the major perks of homeschooling was that I was able to work at my own pace. And while I had taken off many, many months due to my health, I wanted to remain on track to graduate from high school at sixteen. My mom worked with me to develop a schedule, and I put most of my energy into my last few years of high school (saving the rest of my time for practicing instruments and my brand-new YouTube channel) and graduated in May 2008. I wanted to go to the school my sister attended, which was only about forty minutes away, but I knew that none of the medications we had tried so far would be feasible while living away from home. If I was going to live in a college dorm and was not able to be monitored by my parents, I couldn't be medicated like I was at home.

So we made a big decision—I would go to college medication-free.

We decided that my parents would visit frequently, and my sister and I would go home on the weekends. I would have daily check-ins with my mom, work with the school's academic support team, and persist in healthy lifestyle choices regarding vitamins, diet, and physical fitness. And if at any point anyone from my family sensed that I needed a break, I would listen to their wisdom.

And last, I would not suppress my tics.

College was incredible. It was also challenging, overwhelming, and sometimes too much to handle. There was a season around my senior year when I did go on an antidepressant (mostly due to being a college student, a touring artist on the weekends, and recording music on the weekdays, but that's another chapter), and seasons throughout the four years when I saw a counselor.

I didn't suppress my tics, but I also didn't have a lot of close friends, and those two things seemed to work hand in hand. But I *did* make friends and build close bonds with my professors and the academic support team. I kept myself busy by being involved with teams and groups, and I even became a resident advisor for a semester. I sat in the front row in every class, and I often spent twice as long studying as everyone else did. I didn't get invited to hang out with a lot of people, but I found the quiet time in my dorm to be beneficial for writing songs and making videos.

I believe that many of my classmates saw me as weird or simply different, but when I would play at open mic or if one of my YouTube videos started circulating in our small community, I think I started to make sense to them. There was this interesting connection I had with most of the campus: I wasn't a close friend with anyone or remotely understood, but I was safe, content, and free to be myself.

And that's all I wanted: to be myself.

But whether it was in middle school minutes after my diagnosis or during college when I could recite the definitions of my conditions as though I were a neurologist, I struggled with what it meant to "be myself."

I didn't like the life of having excessive and sometimes physically painful tics. But I didn't like suppressing them either. Yet the only option outside of suppression was medication, and I also didn't like that experience. It seemed there was no good option, until I realized what it was that I *really* wanted . . .

I wanted to regain control.

I wanted to be able to do or say something without my body interrupting and doing whatever it wanted. I wanted to have a day when my mind wasn't calling the shots and causing me to say something rhythmic or repetitive that I didn't even want to say.

Never in all my years of praying for healing and begging God to fix things did I once ask Him to make my life perfect or even easy. I wasn't interested in that! And as much as Tourette Syndrome has brought me so much pain and frustration, I can't even remember a time when I specifically asked God to take it away. It may sound crazy, but the unplanned and awkward elements of not being neurotypical make me who I am, and it almost feels odd to think of a life completely without it.

Second Corinthians 12 is written by Paul, an apostle, who was also a teacher. And in this passage he does one of my favorite things, which is teaching from a place of personal experience and allowing his complexities to be used as an example to glorify God. In verse 7 he says, "Therefore, in order to keep me from becoming conceited, I was given a thorn in my flesh," a reference to something that is continuously annoying (likely a physical ailment).

In verses 9 and 10 he continues:

But he said to me, "My grace is sufficient for you, for my power is made perfect in weakness." Therefore I will boast all the more gladly about my weaknesses, so that Christ's power may rest on me. That is why, for Christ's sake, I delight in weaknesses, in insults, in hardships, in persecutions, in difficulties. For when I am weak, then I am strong.

The weaknesses in our lives don't *have* to be our downfall. They don't have to define us. Instead, the challenges we face can be some of the building blocks that lead us to pursuing God in a way that we likely wouldn't have if everything always worked out the way want. When we are weak, we seek our power in God— the *all* powerful—and we no longer have to focus on the imperfect. God's perfect strength takes control instead, and our struggles and our inability to control things become the key ingredients in a recipe for freedom.

But even so, I have prayed to regain control.

I don't want to run everyone's life or become a control freak. I simply want to have the freedom to make my own choices about how my arms and legs move.

When people find out I have Tourette Syndrome, after saying something like . . .

"I would've never known!"

"But you don't curse!"

"Wow, you seem so normal!"

. . . their first question is always a variation of

"What do you do?"

"What are your tics?"

"Can you show me?"

Sometimes it's a new doctor I have, or I might be on a film set and the hairstylist or makeup artist deserves a heads-up. But honestly, one of the most frustrating things in the world is being asked about every aspect of a condition that has taken me twenty-eight years to understand. Because Tourette Syndrome isn't a few silly sounds that I make that people will be intrigued by; it is a daily impact on my life, my schedule, and my emotions.

I can't even walk from point A to point B without check-ing to see if there would be something in my way that might make me trip and fall, because in a moment of stress or a lapse in the ability to suppress, I could find myself in a wrist brace or worse—which has happened more times than I can count.

I have had the incredible privilege to be part of a recent study that adjusts my jaw, which adjusts the neurons that are connected *through* my jaw, which in the long run will help me to have fewer symptoms. And naturally, as most people with my condition get older and pass puberty, we learn to manage on a daily basis in a way that affords a seemingly "normal" or almost neurotypical life.

Even so, I still have Tourette Syndrome. I still have anxiety that triggers it, and I still daily experience having little to no control over my own body.

What Can We Control?

After reading this, you may feel as though you've gained some insight into my life in a way that you didn't have before. How-ever, my life isn't *that* different from yours.

We all have something in our lives that we can't control.

It may not be with your physical body—maybe it's some-thing within your family, like an addiction that has a hold greater than you can understand. Or maybe you find yourself pushing toward a career that is contingent on the "yes" of someone, and it seems like they may answer "no."

Maybe where you live is not somewhere you're proud of, but you know it's your reality for this season. Or maybe you're physically unable to see someone you care about, and you're faced with the pain that you can't see them or touch them or hold them when you want to. Maybe you want to parent a child, but for whatever reason, you're not sure if that can ever happen.

I have no idea what your day to day looks like, but I know there are moments you face that are out of your control.

There are things you try to suppress, that you try to forget about or ignore because you want to feel normal and you want to feel included. But at some point, those things will show up and maybe even show out, and you'll be left trying to pick up the pieces as your reality seems to fall apart.

In that moment, you might realize that your only safe place is your bed . . . your room . . . your home . . . because everywhere else simply seems to attack you.

Or maybe you don't even feel safe in your own home and maybe you spend every day wondering when you'll feel safe again—when you'll feel in control again.

I started speaking publicly when I was nineteen. (Well, I've been speaking for a long time, but in regard to getting paid to be a motivational speaker at an actual event, I was nineteen. ☺) I was the youngest female speaker ever for The Revolve Tour, which was the teen spinoff of a women's conference called Women of Faith. This conference would often draw 10,000 girls per weekend, and after being "discovered" on YouTube by two great people named Katie and Chad, I found myself hired on to the tour to travel and sing, and to share my story.

As we get older, we learn so much more about life and about who we are. And some of our values and morals may even change. But that tour was almost ten years ago, and I can literally quote verbatim the words I used to say onstage, as they will forever remain true.

"I choose to focus on what I can control."

There's so much simplicity in those nine words. But the simplicity holds so much truth.

I cannot control my Tourette Syndrome, yet I *can* make the terrible choice to suppress it and suffer the consequences later.

You cannot control the circumstances of your life, but you *can* choose the folly of denial, to ignore the pain, suppress the feelings you have, and suffer the consequences later.

On the other hand, knowing that I cannot control my Tourette Syndrome, I *can* choose to be grateful for my family, the doctors, and the community God has given me, and lean in to their wisdom, advice, and support.

> *Knowing that I cannot control my Tourette syndrome, I can choose to be grateful for my family, the doctors, and the community God has given me, and lean in to their wisdom, advice, and support.*

Realizing that you cannot control the circumstances of your life, you *can* choose to be grateful for the gifts God has given you, and lean in to community, wisdom, and support too.

There are many things we cannot control. But there are other things simply waiting for us to receive them.

There is joy; there is peace. There is laughter; there is hope. There is rest; there is quiet.

I can control how much I do or don't care about these things. I decide if I want to accept God's joy. It's not about saying that if I have a day without Tourette's tics, I must be having a day full of joy; it's about recognizing that even on the days when my tics are their worst and my body is in constant pain, I can still choose joy.

I don't have to be completely over the hurdle or the circumstance to recognize that there is still a reason to find joy and hope.

Where there is breath—there is hope. And that breath doesn't have to be a soft and consistent one. Some days it may be a heavy and burdened one.

We can't always change our current situation, but our reaction to it has much more of an impact than we realize.

I'm not saying to ignore pain, trust me—I have written a whole chapter on feelings. But I *am* encouraging all of us to take control over what we can.

I know what it means to have little to no control over your body on a day-to-day basis. But I choose to take pride in the things that I can control.

When Aaron and I named our daughter Isabella Brave, I was only a few months pregnant. It was odd, because we had no idea if we were having a boy or a girl. We did have a boy name picked out, but something inside us told us to settle on a girl name first. It was also interesting because initially we intended to wait until she was born to name her, but once we said *Isabella Brave* out loud, there was no going back. That was her name.

As the months went on, people would always ask what we were hoping for. Well-meaning people would ask if we wanted to have a boy or a girl, and if we wanted our child to be an athlete, like my husband, or a musician, like me. But when you're pregnant, you find yourself hearing one sentiment more than any other:

"I just pray you have a healthy baby."

I never want any kind of pain to be a part of my child's life. I'm not interested in seeing her crying and I don't ever want to see her hurting. Even right now, as I'm typing this chapter, she's in the other room with my husband and has been crying for about eleven seconds. She's probably hungry or tired. Also, she's a baby, and babies cry.

It's taking everything within me not to go into the other room. While I know that Aaron, a former daycare teacher and an incredible uncle and father, is fully capable of taking care of her, just to hear her cry for even two seconds is challenging for me.

I don't ever want her to experience pain—but I know that she will.

She is a human, born into an imperfect world because of the choices of humans, and I know that because of this, her life will be full of moments she cannot control. I know that whether it is in regard to her health, emotions, relationships, community, neighborhood, job, or career, she will face things she cannot control.

So while I believe that it is beautiful if your child has great health, I never once prayed for a healthy child.

Instead, I prayed that her name would speak volumes to the kind of person she is and would forever be. I prayed that *brave* would be more than five letters attached to her birth certificate and that she would be full of courage to face whatever life throws her way.

My husband and I specifically prayed for a child who would be full of joy, so that no matter what, she would be full of the joy of the Lord and fully capable of dancing in every single storm.

We prayed for hope. Peace. And we prayed that she would be a person of faith, choosing to press in to God's promises in both the joyful and tumultuous times.

Maybe it's because I was never a healthy kid—and I certainly wasn't a healthy baby—that I don't put health on a pedestal. I just don't live a life that assumes that without physical health, you are less than or not a good representation of what God can do in your life.

A Different Kind of Control Freak

I understand that every single one of us has something in our lives that we cannot control, but through the gifts God gives us, we can find our healing.

I'm unsure as to what my complete physical healing looks like. I'm unsure if it will even be on this side of heaven. But I do know that by choosing to live in the boldness of who I am, I am embracing who God made me to be.

Every day I make the choice to be bold about what makes me different. Whether in a particular season my tics are diminished or exceptionally significant, my circumstance is a part of my everyday, and I make the choice to embrace that—even if it looks different from what everyone else would expect.

I used to wake up overwhelmed at the idea of trying to control my day to day, but now I have shifted my focus to controlling elements of my character to impact my circumstances, instead of the other way around.

And maybe, in a way that's different from the insult, I *am* a control freak.

Control / noun /
    the power to **influence** or direct people's **behavior** or the course of **events**

Freak / noun /
    a very unusual and unexpected event or situation

FINDING QUIET

Maybe I look at the world around me—seeing the brokenness that every single one of us faces—and my heart is heavy. I face the fact that I simply cannot control certain events and situations.

But maybe, in a very **unusual and unexpected** way, I'm embracing the power to **influence my own behavior**. And if you're anything like me and have a complicated relationship with control, I want you to join me as we figure out the choices to make that allow us to find freedom.

In the event of pain, choose patience.
In the event of weeping, choose joy.
In the event of hatred, choose love.
In the event of war, choose peace.
In the event of destruction, choose to build.
In the event of brokenness, choose to mend.

Maybe it's not about forcing the pain, tears, hatred, war, destruction, and brokenness to go away.

Maybe it's about welcoming the long-suffering, joy, love, peace, intention, and efforts to mend so that they are much louder.

seven

Plans and Dreams

When Aaron and I found out that we were expecting, we immediately jumped into planning mode. We had already talked about having kids—we wanted to have a big family. While we had enough space for us and a child, maybe even two, and our car was functional, we decided to look into moving to a bigger house and adding a more family-friendly car.

I really wanted a car that could seat seven. And not in a way that said, "Oh! My car has two rows and there happens to be a third one we could use sometimes." I wanted a full-sized SUV that could seat seven people: two adults and five kids of varying ages.

I wanted to make sure the car would accommodate a growing family. As our kids got older, I wanted to have something that made sense for soccer practice and carpooling with their friends, that was also either hybrid or fully electric so we could transport a lot of kids and reduce our carbon footprint at the same time. I also wanted to make sure there was a ton of trunk space, so if all the kids were with me and I was going to the grocery store, I could fit all the groceries in the back, and maybe even a stroller, in case I still needed one by that point.

Then there was the house. There was no doubt that it needed to have at least five bedrooms—maybe even six. It's not because I wanted to live in a big house; I wanted to make sure we would have enough space for all of our children, and that our home would be adequate in case we might want to be foster parents someday. I already knew exactly what kind of dream kitchen I wanted, plus there needed to be an outdoor playing area, a homeschool room for the older kids, and a playroom for the younger ones.

Lists usually give me a lot of peace for the things I've already accomplished and get me excited about the things I need to do, but for some reason, every time it came down to talking about adding a family car, or where we would live and what kind of house we would either rent or buy, I found myself becoming increasingly stressed out. A few months into being pregnant, I decided that I didn't want to make any more plans with the exception of what to pack in my hospital bag. Deep down I wanted to keep searching for a new car and house, but I told Aaron that it was becoming an overwhelming task that consumed my every thought, and I didn't know where to go from there.

That weekend my friend Kristin happened to be visiting from the East Coast. Kristin was not only my maid of honor, but our friendship has evolved into a sisterhood over the years. We've walked with each other through some of the lowest lows but also the most incredible highs. Every time we talk, the conversation is full of joy and realness, and oftentimes we don't even have to talk to know what's on the other one's mind.

Kristin and I went out for lunch, and on the car ride back to my house, I was telling her that I was thinking of getting a "mom car" but was also starting to doubt my decision because the process was starting to feel like too much. She asked me what kind of cars I had been looking at, so I told her about one of the options, which was a mini SUV. It was super safe, had all of the family car qualifications, and was in our price range.

I had become so consumed with making plans for the future that I lost the ability to embrace the present.

But then I started talking about full-sized SUVs with a third row. I told her how I wanted to be prepared for when we added more kids to our family, and how that was even having an impact on how I was searching for a house. I told her that it had almost become a scenario of all-or-nothing when it came to the car, because it didn't feel right to get something for *now* when I could be prepared for *later*.

Then Kristin, in a way that only a dear friend could (and in a way I absolutely needed), shut me down—quickly.

She asked, "Don't you think that if you have a bigger car, you'll only be adding pressure to yourself to fill it up?"

Much like my counselor questioning my habitual interview listening, I can't promise that was Kristin's question verbatim. But I knew that my answer was a resounding "Yes!"—which let me know that I needed to make some changes.

I realized that I had not only been doing that with the car, but I had also been doing that with the house. I had become so consumed with making plans for the future that I lost the ability to embrace the present.

There's nothing wrong with planning ahead. There's nothing wrong with having your dream house or your dream car by thirty-five or twenty-one or even eighteen. But I wasn't working toward a dream. I was obsessing over a plan and trying to have so much of tomorrow figured out that I had moments of forgetting to think about today. I was so concerned with trying to see what our lives would be like if we have three or more children that I was too overwhelmed to sit in the present and process that we were about to have our *first* one!

And trust me—when she arrived? It was the second greatest day of my life (first, #wedding). All I wanted to think about was that exact moment. All I wanted to do was sit in the hospital room with my husband and with our child and think about nothing else. I didn't care if our car seated four people, had two doors, or was a fifteen-passenger van. All that mattered in that moment was that whatever car it was, the three of us could be in it together.

I didn't care that we would quickly, much sooner than anticipated, outgrow our quaint, near-the-ocean apartment. It didn't matter that our second bedroom was half recording studio and half nursery. I wasn't consumed with which area would be the playroom and if we could figure out a classroom. All that mattered was that our home was our home, and that the people I love know they have a place in it.

There's so much beauty in dreaming and believing for the future—in hoping and praying for our plans to work out beautifully as we find peace in dreaming up structure and carving out logistics to make our lives, and our loved ones', run as smoothly as possible.

But I've come to understand that there's something just as beautiful when living in the moment and choosing to celebrate whatever that might look like. Even if it's different from what you originally anticipated, I promise there is joy to be found.

In my early twenties, I became an independent artist again. (I was indie for the first few years of my career, then with a record label from ages nineteen to twenty-four, and eventually reached a point where I knew it would be the best decision to be an indie artist again.)

I spent the first few months of my independence writing and recording as much as I could. Even though I would often start feeling nervous or even insecure about sharing music in a completely new way, I still found refuge in creating. I worked with producers and songwriters I had always wanted to work with, and I also closed myself in my room for hours on end to write the vulnerable lyrics I wasn't sure I could ever share. It didn't take long until I started to feel like myself again.

My manager and I welcomed a few new people onto the team to help with upcoming projects, and one of their first suggestions was that I consider pitching my new songs to record labels. I wasn't sure if I ever wanted to sign a record deal again, but I was open to whatever made sense for my career, and ultimately wanted to ensure I would have the opportunity to continue creating and sharing music. Within weeks of telling them this, I had meetings scheduled with the biggest record labels in town.

Suddenly what seemed like a *maybe* in my mind became the source of my hope. I had unfinished but heartfelt demos, fully produced pop tracks, some duets with my sister that I knew had solid lyrics and harmonies, and I even took my guitar *just in case* they wanted to hear something live.

Most of the label executives we met with were friendly and familiar faces. I had been on tours with their artists before, so we had crossed paths backstage or even at awards shows. They were familiar with my music and my style and had seen me play live, but I still wanted to plan as much as I could to make a great impression.

And I promise, I tried.

They were encouraging and supportive about my music that they knew from the radio and the performances they had seen in previous years. They asked questions about my future goals and expressed interest in my ideas. And when I played them my new songs, they enjoyed them.

In the first meeting, I specifically remember seeing their faces light up at certain musical changes or lyrics, and thanking them when they shared how much they enjoyed certain songs and said they couldn't wait to hear more. And there was no underlying *We didn't like that—do you have anything else?* There was genuine interest in the music I was playing, to the point that they were curious if there were more where those songs came from.

In the second meeting, my solo songs were not that much of a hit. I felt bad because one song, "Party Like A Princess," was a hit in its own way—as in, the track hit so hard with the bass it literally busted the speakers in their main office. I realized we should probably go a different route, and I decided to play them the demos that my sister and I wrote and recorded together.

There was a shift in the room.

They loved it.

They asked for the stories behind the songs, our potential timeline for fully producing them, and if we had enough for a full-length album. Morgan and I were trying to be subtle about the hope that was stirring, but I remember making eye contact with her and, for a moment, it seemed like things may look very different than we thought, in a really good way.

As my sister and I, our manager, and the other guys from our team walked to our cars in the parking lot, we exchanged excited commentary about the completely different yet positive reactions from both meetings. There were phrases going around like, "Oh, they will definitely offer something before the year is out," and, "We'll basically get to choose which one we want!"

As the weeks progressed, we were copied on email correspondence from more labels. Our demos were emailed around, and the new members of our team were more hopeful than ever.

The plan was working.

We had not only procured the highly coveted meetings with high-profile executives, but we received responses that led us to believe contracts and offers would be rolling in before we knew it.

Just months before this, I wasn't sure I ever wanted to have these conversations or even consider being anything but indie. But all of a sudden I was feeling confident about the future and began to actively make plans for what my tomorrow could look like.

I was living in Atlanta at the time, and I started to think about moving to Nashville. I had lived in Nashville before, and while I love the food and my friends who live there, God had previously made it clear to me that Tennessee wasn't my home. But I wanted to make sure that wasn't exclusive to the past, so I started to consider and pray about whether God would have Tennessee be a part of my future.

I also reached out to friends who knew the ins and outs of my story. I asked them to pray about the potentially endless possibilities that could be arising. I told them about the overwhelmingly positive and exciting meetings and emails.

Though different from what I originally anticipated, maybe this plan is going to work out, I thought.

We prayed and waited for responses from the record labels day after day. There were occasional conference calls from time to time with my manager and/or my sister to assure each other that this was all part of the waiting game. The days turned into weeks and eventually the weeks turned into months, and the answer was obvious.

I never knew quiet could be so loud.

Where it was deemed appropriate, I reached out to follow up, but there was literal silence on all ends. There were no phone calls or even emails. The interest that was once there seemed to be gone, and the plan that my team had set in place had completely fallen apart.

Plans Unmade

I don't like the idea of sitting down and dreaming and planning, only to find out that none of those things will come to fruition. I was annoyed that we spent so much time in the stages of hoping, and also a bit embarrassed that I allowed myself to be vulnerable enough to share that hope with others.

Why did I go to the meetings? I bet they're all laughing at me now.

Why did I ask my friends to pray? Now they'll ask for updates and I'll have to tell them it didn't work out.

Why did I start planning about moving or marketing with the support of a label? Now it's not happening and I've only wasted my time.

The recovery process after failed or diverted plans can often be long and dramatic for me. I become insecure about the excitement I was engaged in and want to crawl into a hole, investing solely in isolation, until everyone has forgotten about me. Only then will I reemerge as a new person who is free from the sign on her forehead that seems to read *Jamie Grace failed—again.*

As I'm continually learning and growing, I have made the conscious decision to step away from my unhealthy desire to completely isolate myself. I'm not saying that it's easy (it's the polar opposite), but when I work toward making daily decisions a routine choice, they gradually become natural habits.

Each day I have the choice to run into the hidden, dark corners of my home and mind that feed off negative thoughts and failed plans.

Or

I can push myself to make the choices that motivate me to step into the light and the quiet, where true peace is found.

So how do we push ourselves even when our plans are falling apart? How do we pursue positive thoughts and emotional progression when our mind tells us that it's no longer worth it? How do we recover after a diversion of our plans that makes us feel like our dreams no longer matter?

I have found assurance in a surprising way: by simply stating the obvious, like pointing out a hot-pink elephant in the room.

My dreams won't always come true. My plans won't always work out.

It sounds negative. Truly. And my natural team-hype personality is much more pro-positivity than anything, but I have actually found a significant amount of hope, courage, and even drive to keep pushing on in saying those things out loud to myself.

When I was a kid, my dreams and aspirations reached further than any eye could see. I wanted to work with monkeys in the circus, I wanted to be an astronaut, and I wanted to be an actress and a singer. As I got older, my dreams became less and less about my future career, and I started to focus on the kind of woman I wanted to be and the kind of family I wanted to have.

The main dream that remained on my heart was to be married by my early twenties and have a few kids by the time I was twenty-five. In reality, at twenty-five, I was super single (we're talking never-held-hands-with-a-guy kinda single). As a Georgia resident at the time, I was actually pursuing the steps to becoming a foster mom, but just after my twenty-fifth birthday (the age requirement for unmarried applicants), my family moved to California. I was excited about the move, but in some ways it felt like a slap in the face. I knew I couldn't determine when and how (or if) my future husband would show up, but becoming a foster or adoptive mom was something that took a *ton* of planning, and within weeks of meeting the age minimum, those plans fell apart.

The dream of becoming a wife and/or mom by twenty-five never came true.

When we have dreams—whether for our career, hobbies, family, or education—and they don't come true, we oftentimes become very discouraged and want to give up. We can get to a place of self-doubt and insecurity, and it can be *so* hard to recover. But when we face the fact that all of our dreams and plans simply won't happen, we can take preventative measures for our own emotional stability.

Try this. I know it feels crazy, and maybe it seems a bit too negative for a book whose goal is to be encouraging, but try saying this:

My dreams won't always come true. My plans won't always work out.

> When we face the fact that all of our dreams and plans simply won't happen, we can take preventative measures for our own emotional stability.

By saying that simple mantra, you're allowing yourself the freedom for *things* to potentially fall, all while knowing that *you* are not a failure. You're accepting that sometimes things simply don't work out, but it doesn't mean that *you* are not worthy of trying again.

You may not get an offer from every job you apply to or get accepted into every college that receives your beautifully penned essay(s). You may not get engaged or married when you thought you would or have a child by the time you're a certain age. You may not get the car you want or the house you've always dreamed of, and trust me—not only is it possible you won't get a record deal, you may not even get a call back.

But if you allow it, the dreams and plans, whether diverted or dissolved, can teach you more about hope and potential than any accomplishment ever will.

Planning with an Open Hand

We ended up getting a family car that has *somewhat* of a third row. It's certainly not a full-sized SUV like I originally planned, and if anyone over 5 feet 8 is trying to sit back there, I want them to know that I will pray for them on the ride.

And by the time we had our sweet Isabella? We hadn't moved. We allowed ourselves to embrace our humble first place as a family, and when she was six months old and we physically couldn't fit her toys and our couch in the living room, then we packed up a rented truck and made the move.

And last, I never signed a record deal, and to this day have yet to hear back from any of the labels who previously seemed interested. But I've fallen more in love with being an indie artist than ever before, and I have been humbled by seeing God move in my music in ways that I couldn't have ever imagined, dreamed, or planned.

Sometimes my plans work out almost perfectly. I have my magnetic dry-erase board with my printouts attached, PDFs that I've emailed, and sometimes even audio recordings of meetings with my team. I am blown away by seeing my dreams come to fruition.

But *most* of the time: **My dreams don't always come true. My plans don't always work out.**

What could be seen as a negative has become the realistic stepping-stone for me to embrace imperfection, and I hope you can embrace it too. Together, we can make our plans and set our goals for our everyday lives and our long-term ideals. *Then* we can work hard, pray more, and dream big, knowing that in the end, the plans that need to surface will, and the lessons learned and the joy that is found will always be worth it.

FINDING QUIET

It's easy to fill the silence with noise that overpowers the insecurities shouting our names. It's easy to plan over and over again instead of letting go of a dream. But if you press in to the quiet moments when the emails aren't coming, the phone isn't ringing, the text messages and DMs are going unread and unnoticed, and conversations don't exist, you would be surprised at the three things that could happen.

One: The Journey

Ohhh, the beautiful cliché that celebrates enjoying the journey as opposed to becoming consumed with the destination. Every broken and burdened element of your journey is part of leading you where you need to be. Despite every wrong turn that the GPS attempts to recalculate, you will still end up at your final destination.

The twists, turns, and turbulence can either break or build you, and that choice is up to you.

It's okay to feel broken and it's okay to hurt. There's something significant about knowing how and when to sit and cry, and when to invite or allow your friends and family to hold you and cry with you. You should never, ever allow your pain to go unnoticed or your weeping to feel insignificant. You should instead press in to the angst that is building and plead that your frustration turn into a desire for a deep breath and a fresh start.

I am hardwired to believe that my joy wouldn't be joy if I didn't experience pain first. Psalm 30:5 says, "Weeping may stay for the night, but rejoicing comes in the morning." How could that verse embrace the joy if it didn't begin with accepting the night that is full of weeping?

While we're in the thick of a storm, it can seem impossible to believe that there is hope on the other side. But there is no sunrise without a sunset and no victory without a fight. Speak into your broken moments that there *will* be a brighter day, and embrace the journey in every step.

Two: The Lesson

You start to ask yourself:
What can I learn from this?
How can I grow from this experience?
What can I do better next time?
Instead of being consumed with how things didn't work out, see them as tools to make adjustments for the future so that you don't run into the same predicaments as before. Start to reevaluate your methods and practices and, in the process, learn and grow from choices or decisions that were

possibly mistakes, mishaps, or simply something worth trying in a different way.

This turns your

I wish I could've . . . into *Next time I can* . . .
If only I would've . . . into *In the future, I will* . . .
Why didn't I just . . . into *This time I choose to* . . .

You're acknowledging the past instead of avoiding it, and taking intentional steps toward how you will operate in the future.

Three: The New

You could, almost immediately, start trying to figure out ways to create new dreams to build on—or apart from—the ones that didn't happen. To create something *new*—a new vision, a new passion. You'll find yourself with *new* mercies and a *new* kind of joy because yesterday's story isn't being told anymore.

Your thoughts are no longer filled with who you could have been and what you could have done, and you are not consumed with what could happen and who you could be. The past isn't your enemy and the future isn't your obsession. You start to live in the now, in the present, and to find and create the new in every moment.

eight

Competition vs. Community

I've always had somewhat of an obsession with soccer. Tim Howard is a famous goalie. He also has Tourette Syndrome and has always been a great inspiration to me. I also remember seeing Mia Hamm on a cereal box when I was little and being convinced that girls really could do anything.

I've always found soccer not only fun to watch, but also fun to play. I love it so much that I started a soccer league when I was about seven or eight years old. Please note that I didn't say I started a soccer *team* or joined a soccer *team*.

I attempted to start an entire soccer league.

I made a poster (yes, one) to put up in my neighborhood to announce tryouts. And when I realized there wasn't anywhere in my neighborhood to post it, I simply kept it with me at all times to show anyone I crossed paths with. Reasonable.

My goal was to have various teams within the league, and to eventually find a way to afford uniforms and trophies, and maybe even someday go to the Olympics and win a ton of medals.

As you can probably imagine, it was an epic fail. It started to crumble when nobody showed up for the tryouts, with the exception of me, but believe it or not, I still decided to pursue the league.

I set up chairs that would be my goalies and constantly played soccer in the backyard—by myself. (And with the occasional neighbor who joined me from time to time.)

It sounds a lot sadder than it was, because even though it wasn't what I anticipated, all I really wanted was to be part of a team. And even though I technically wasn't, my seven-year-old self had dreams that were *so* big it still somehow felt like I was finally a part of a soccer team. It didn't matter that my main teammate was myself or that my neighbors only played with me sporadically. I loved soccer, had created a "league," and genuinely found joy in that.

I joined an *actual* soccer team my senior year of high school. I've never been exceptionally athletic, but my parents were able to find an indoor recreational co-ed team that you didn't have to try out for, so it was right up my alley. I should point out that I was possibly the worst player on the team, and I'm curious if they ever rethought the anyone-can-sign-up policy after they saw me play.

I had a ton of fun being a part of the team, and I even assisted in one goal! I also have a memory of scoring one, but it's very possible that's just a memory I made up to make myself feel better.

But honestly, the reality of not being Player of the Year and sitting on the bench most of the time, just like in my childhood "league," wasn't that sad. I enjoyed getting to run around with my teammates before the games, talk about the game afterward, drink Gatorade, and spend time with them. I didn't care that I wasn't scoring the most points, if any at all. I just wanted to be a part of the team.

Fast-forward to a year later: I was a freshman in college, and I realized this could finally be my chance to join a *real* soccer team. Not an indoor, recreational league, but a team with tryouts, a full-time coach, rules, *and* fifteen-passenger vans that took you to games in neighboring states.

I already knew the coach and a lot of the players because my sister had played on the team two years prior. So after a conversation about my past athletic experience and a general understanding of my abilities and passions in life . . .

Let's just say I didn't end up with a jersey.

But the coach knew about my passion for videography and production, and I became the team's official videographer. I stood on the sidelines taking photos and videos of notable moments. The team also used my video footage as a game tape to watch and take notes for improvement. Or so I thought.

On my first overnight trip with the team, I wanted to show them the game tape right away instead of turning it in to the coach. Unfortunately, I forgot proper cables to hook my camera up to the TV in the hotel, so I wasn't able to show it. The girls weren't too bummed about it, which I initially assumed was because they were pretty tired from the game.

But I soon realized that they hadn't been watching any of the game tapes.

And they really didn't need the footage.

Truth be told, I wasn't technically needed. At all.

It would seem that would be the worst thing for someone to hear. But for some reason, that was one of the best things for me. Because I realized that even though I wasn't needed, I was chosen. And even though I thought that I was on the team for one reason, God *still* used me in amazing ways, and that wasn't something I took for granted.

I was almost like a mascot or a cheerleader, cheering them on from the sidelines and encouraging them on long drives to and from games. And while my game tapes weren't used by the team, I started posting their highlights of great passes or saves on social media for their family members and friends to see. I would often take my guitar on trips, and when we were stuck in traffic or bummed at a gas station on the road back home after a tough loss, I would sing songs, take requests, and try to make them laugh. My friend Liz loves to remind me that one of the songs I used to play for them was called "Hold Me."

It was never about being the best, the fastest, or the strongest. It was always about finding my place on a team, being a part of seeing something greater than me.

My entire life I knew that soccer was about competition. I knew that the goal of the game was to win. But somehow every time I found myself having any type of involvement with a soccer team, I learned that competition was nowhere to be found. It was never about being the best, the fastest, or the strongest. It was always about finding my place on a team, being a part of seeing something greater than me.

The Gift of Not Competing

My freshman year of college, the year of becoming a soccer videographer, was also the year I became *Jamie Grace*. While I was named Jamie Grace Harper at birth, and have introduced myself by just my first and middle names since I was seven, it wasn't until my freshman year of college that I began to be *known* as the singer Jamie Grace. That year I got my first job on a TV show, booked my first national tour, and went into the studio to record an EP.

Soccer season was ending as I started making weekly trips to Nashville for work, but I took the same mindset of community and teamwork into the entertainment industry. Only to realize—quickly—that was not the norm.

Maybe it was my naïveté, or maybe it was just my hope for something more, but I didn't know that the real world was all about competition. I always saw success as coinciding with how well your community was thriving: We were doing *well* in life when we were loved and showing love, and our careers and academic achievements were merely bonuses.

But I started to learn that success to other people, *many* people, was making sure that *you* were the one thriving.

I remember when I was first nominated for a Grammy Award. Everyone kept saying that I was going to win, that I was going to take it home, and that I was going to kill it! Why? Because I'm the best, they said, and *my* song is the best.

But I didn't like the pressure of being the best.

And I didn't like the pressure of having to win!

I was excited enough about the nomination; I didn't want to keep pushing to have *everything*. In my mind, I kept thinking about the people I was nominated alongside and wondering, *What if it's* their *turn to be the best? If* I'm *always the best, does no one else get a chance?*

I remember sitting in a studio session once, wanting to add a ukulele to a song I was recording, but the producers said no. I had been playing ukulele for a few years and had even landed a sponsorship with a company that makes them, but I wasn't allowed to put one on a song on my album.

Why?

They told me there was another female artist with a song on the radio whose song was ukulele driven. The producers drove the point home:

That's her thing—you have to find the thing that makes you stand out.

It's not that I didn't want to stand out. But I didn't like the feeling of standing out just to push ahead. I wanted to be part of a community, not a competition, but it seemed like it was impossible to have one without the other.

I've had multiple conversations with young women my age who make music both stylistically similar to my own and vastly different from what I do. And I've been told by these women— who I'm positive have not talked to each other—some of the most disturbing things. When my songs were reaching number one on the radio, and when my songs were charting the highest on the charts, their managers and their producers sat them down and told them, "She is your competition. This is what you're striving for."

I'll never forget the time a tour-mate looked me in the eye and told me that her manager said that until she was doing as well as Jamie Grace, she wasn't doing well at all.

Her words sank so deep that I didn't even know how to react. At the beginning of that tour, I thought we could be friends; I thought we could build something like a sisterhood. But I was nothing but competition to her, and while she could have chosen to be my friend, it could potentially have been at the expense of her career.

―――――――

Conversations like those would often be the starting point of my rethinking everything.

Before becoming friends with anyone or even having coffee with someone new, I found myself thinking, *Are they my competition? Is this a competition? Do I need to work harder to be like them? Do I need to work harder at standing out?*

It's no secret that this world often pits women against each other, and as a result, so many of us feel like we are in constant competition with other women, including our friends and sisters. But here are three times I learned to go beyond keeping score and make friends with other women, even when they are doing things that are similar to what I do.

1. My friend Melinda Doolittle is one of the most talented singers I know. While we have different styles as far as our music and the way we perform it, we are both artists who, on paper, may seem too similar to be friends. Yet when it comes to conversations about our careers or exciting moments in our personal lives, we find ourselves on FaceTime for a significantly long time.

   I visited Melinda in the studio when she was recording her most recent project, and on my first headlining tour, she was the first friend to come by our rehearsals. There was even a time when we had some of the same people on our professional teams. In a culture and an industry that would encourage us to keep our distance, the things that make us similar have become the foundation for what makes her one of my closest friends. And now that relationship continues through generations, as she is Isabella's godmother.

2. My internet friend Victory [Boyd], turned real-life friend, turned internet friend again (because she and I both travel so much it's nearly impossible to keep track of each other) sings and plays guitar. She's a solo artist who writes her own songs but also writes for other artists *and* sings with her siblings as well. The first time we had dinner together, I was pretty blown away to hear that she felt like we had grown up together, as she was inspired by my music in her childhood and teen years.

    Beyond music, Victory and I are both black girls who write, sing, and play guitar. She told me that over the years, because of our similarities, people have told her that she reminds them of me. We both laughed it off because we're used to the concept of comparison. But neither of us is willing to allow comparison to be the barrier to friendship.

3. I recently sang for the sweet-sixteen party of a girl who is a fan of my music. I was honored not only to sing for her and her friends, but to be the surprise guest and see their excited faces and hear their joyous screams as the birthday girl's dad announced me. I sat on a barstool in

the living room and invited the birthday girl and her friends to choose which songs I would sing next. I had a backup set list just in case, but I wanted it to be more interactive. (At a house party celebrating my twenty-first birthday, two of my friends had done the same thing for me, and it was one of the most humbling things I have ever been part of, and it led to a lasting experience for my friends and me.) I wanted to do the same for this girl. As I was singing, she also started to sing a little. I stumbled over the second verse of a song she wanted to hear (it was an old-school one!), and as I noticed that she knew the words, I leaned over to listen to her sing—to "cheat." Turns out, she was an incredible singer. I even took a moment to say, "Wait! Do you sing?" And her friends all screamed, "Yes! Yes!" She knew the words. And I could have easily said "Thanks" and continued to sing the ones she had given me. But in that moment I thought, *Why would I sing it all by myself when I could share the spotlight?* I chose the latter. And she sang it much better than I ever could have.

These friendships, relationships, and moments *are the way* we combat competition. Choosing *not* to compete with the people who would be deemed our competition is one of the best ways we can boldly live out love and community in a culture that promotes the opposite.

Instead of similarities being the foundation for competition, let those similarities be what drives a friendship.

If I could go back and tell newly professional singer-songwriter Jamie Grace anything about competition, I would tell her these three things:

1. There will always be someone who wants to pit you against someone else, but you don't have to let that stop you from making friends.
2. Choose collaboration over competition.
3. Make friends with people who are like you *and* different from you.

Don't Keep Score

Ecclesiastes 4:4–6 in the New Living Translation says,

> "Then I observed that most people are motivated to
> success because they envy their neighbors. But this,
> too, is meaningless—like chasing the wind.
> 'Fools fold their idle hands,
> leading them to ruin.'
> And yet,
> 'Better to have one handful with quietness
> than two handfuls with hard work
> and chasing the wind.'"

To pursue a career or a dream, to pursue any kind of success out of being competitive with or envious of someone is meaningless. The Bible says that it's better to live in quiet than to work hard at things that are meaningless.

For me, playing soccer was never about keeping score—and that's why I wanted to play. But whether your hobby, job, or sport is competitive or not, it is our *lives* that we have to keep in check. And in life, the less I keep score, the less I'll worry about how others are stacked up against me.

The less you keep score in your own life, the less you'll worry about how others are stacked up against you.

The more you focus on why you do what you do, the more you are able to be a better version of yourself without even having enough time to see how your ranking compares to anyone else.

I've had moments when my songs were #1 on the charts. There was even a season when an original song of mine was simultaneously charting in two separate genres—only the second time that exact charting had been done (and it was around ten years prior). It felt amazing. I was so honored that people were listening to my music and that radio stations felt compelled to play it that much.

The less I keep score, the less I'll worry about how others are stacked up against me.

Yet there was a moment when that song became #2. Then #3, eventually dropping out of the top 100. And as much as we can feel good when our accomplishments are at the highest heights, our level of contentment on the other end is what truly defines our character.

I can genuinely say that in the moments of having multiple #1 hits and the moments of having no songs climbing the charts, I am still grateful. I have had moments of worry and moments of doubt, but ultimately, I know that I am still pushing toward being who I was called to be and continuing to create what I was called to create.

FINDING QUIET

If you're the girl who can't help but notice that her grades are always a little lower than her sister's, or the wife who feels like she can't compete with all the other moms her age, or the guy who worries he'll never make his parents as proud as his siblings have, this is for you:

You were not made to be her.

She was not made to be you.

You were not made to be him.

He was not made to be you.

I know these things are easier to say than to believe, but all I ask is that you say it daily until you believe it. I ask that you sing it, scream it, or even draw it on a Post-it Note and stick it to your bathroom mirror. Allow yourself to find the rhythm in those phrases so that it feels like a morning mantra!

Only I can do what I was called to do.

Only I can be who I was made to be.

Only I can create what I was called to create.

Only I can live the life that I was created to live.

Many of my songs that are upbeat and sound like a melodic version of cotton candy and a bubble gum forest were written during some of the darkest times of my life. My song "One of a Kind" has the bounciest bounce of the peppiest piano, and every lyric came from a prayer offered when the neck of my shirt was drenched in tears.

I remember telling God about all the things that made me feel less-than or insecure. I opened up about the parts of my life that I honestly wasn't proud of, and then I started to get insecure about that! I started to realize that everything I was praying about, everything that made me feel isolated, wasn't *that* unique. I started to realize that almost everyone could pray that same prayer, and I was worried I was wasting God's time (not possible).

As I started praying about the fact that I was getting insecure about praying about the fact that I was feeling insecure (yep!), God gave me the words to the chorus . . .

> *To You, I'm one of a kind*
> *You look at me and say, "She's mine"*
> *To You, I'm not as crazy as I think*

God began speaking into my life that whether I feel like I'm ten steps behind or I'm running too close a race with everyone else, I'm *His*. And He doesn't create carbon copies or duplicate demos of people, waiting until we inevitably find our identical match somewhere in the world. Even identical twins have differences, because that's how intentional our God is when He creates.

He didn't create us to compete against each other. He has given us all gifts and talents that enable us to thrive individually even when we come together! It's incredible what we can do.

I spent many years struggling to find balance. I wanted to thrive as a businesswoman who owned a production company creating honest music and inspiring art that *wasn't* founded on the principle of competing with others just to get ahead. I never wanted to chase the wind.

I know that many of us feel this way, wanting to embrace originality, yet we feel caught up by the world's standard of being original, which seems to be rooted in pushing ahead just to prove how original you really are.

That mindset can cause us to doubt our goals . . . our relationships . . . our intentions and the intentions of others. So much so that we might think about giving up and walking away.

But as we press in to who we were called to be—who God created us to be—and we keep our focus solely on pursuing *that* as our main goal? We're able to live a life as a carefree kid in the backyard playing soccer with a handful of quiet.

nine

Friends, Frenemies, and Forced Quiet

I love sleepovers. Ever since I was a kid, I've always found that there's something incredible about inviting a bunch of friends over to embrace sweatpants, messy hair, and watching a bunch of movies while eating a bunch of random food. As an adult I'm somewhat of a health nut on most days, but I have no shame ordering a ton of pizza and making (or *baking*) the most of frozen buffalo chicken boneless wings.

I love my friends. I love late nights. I love connecting with a movie in an emotional way and crying way too much while simultaneously laughing —confused and content with all my mixed feelings.

I feel like movie nights really became somewhat of a thing around middle or high school. They were previously called sleepovers, then movie nights, and as I became a teen, they were simply girls' nights. Most girls I knew would spend girls' nights painting each other's nails and having a homemade spa, but I really didn't have time for that. I just wanted the buffalo wings and the movie(s).

Nonetheless, I made it work. A lot of the girls I grew up with didn't necessarily know much about hair or skin products that were suitable for my complexion and hair texture, so while they did their thing, I would just watch the movie, eat the snacks, and sit in the joy that I genuinely felt to simply be included.

For a while, I thought I was surrounded by an incredible community. But there was a point when I started to realize that some of these girls who seemed like good friends were actually mean girls. There was one girl in particular I was close with as a teenager. I would have even dared to say that she was my best friend at one point. One of the main reasons we were best friends was because we were so similar, which seems like a harmless reason, and even a great one, to pick a friend, but it in our case it wasn't.

Both of us had chosen the Christian faith for ourselves at a young age, and we were really proud of that. We had so much in common when it came to the way we viewed the Bible and the world, so I assumed that was the foundation of our friendship. But as we got older, I realized that we weren't friends because of our Christian faith. I realized that she took her Christian faith as a way to be boastful and prideful. And not in who God is, but in who *she* was because of her choices.

When we spent time with other girls, we smiled and joked and told stories. We propped our cameras up on bookshelves, set the self-timer, and rushed to get into the frame to take silly photos together (this was the '90s-kid version of a selfie). We had girls' nights with other girls and stayed up late telling elaborate versions of our most embarrassing moments and quoting our favorite PG movies from beginning to end. Even though we may have been more traditional in some of our beliefs and morals than the other girls we knew, we put those differences aside and were able to create memories and moments that fifteen years later I can still recall.

But when we were alone, everything changed. Our conversations changed to center around the girls we knew who were *different*. It was like a switch flipped the second the other girls' sleeping bags were packed and they were in their moms' minivans. Suddenly, my friend thought it was the perfect time to talk about everything the other girls confided in us. She gossiped to her mom about who was overeating and who was dating someone they shouldn't be. She made arrogant remarks about who was being physically intimate with whom, and revealed the other girls' family secrets.

I remember being uncomfortable and insecure, worried that if I spoke up I would sound like I was judging my friend, but if I stayed silent it would seem like I was condoning their gossip. And while it wasn't my intention to be an enabler of spreading rumors, my silence wasn't helping refute them either. I figured that it was one thing to hold your friends accountable to be loving, humble, and kind. But I didn't even know how to begin to hold an adult accountable as she mocked the very kids who were just in her home. And a part of me was also afraid of not fitting in. I didn't want to be the preacher's daughter who chose to speak up and defend people who weren't even there. So I chose silence. I chose to focus on not making eye contact. And I chose to say "wow" as randomly and quietly as possible, out of fear of seeming like a prude.

I quickly realized that they talked about sin as though they were the cure. Their conversation of temptation made it seem as though they were the ones who decided where grace applied. Initially I thought that all of the conversations we had about our morals and values were an exciting way to find common ground, but I didn't realize that our confidence was at the expense of someone else's weakness.

I started distancing myself from this friend. I became insecure about the fact that I had thought she was a good friend and that our friendship was genuine. I learned that she was using her moral standard to tear others down. If that was the way she treated the people in her own community, why would our friendship be any different? How did I know that she was someone I could trust? What about all the secrets I had told her—even the "small" ones? Did she and her mom sit around laughing about me when I was gone too?

I remember another friendship that I really believed in. For most preacher's kids it can be hard to build a bond with someone in the church, but I did. And we did almost everything together.

We had sleepovers. We emailed each other (way back before the days of FaceTime and texting). There were many moments when I was convinced that she would be my best friend forever.

But we had what today might be called a "fake friendship." When we were near each other we'd hang out, or if we were both online we'd instant-message. She wasn't a terrible person; in fact, she was a lot of fun, and we genuinely had some great times together. But ultimately, she saw me as "beneath" her, and there was no assurance that she would be friendly toward me. But in my desperation to have a BFF, just as in every sitcom filmed in front of a live studio audience, I continuously overlooked the negative.

I knew she was a mean girl all along. But I was so desperate for a friend that I didn't care.

She thought that I was lame and awkward, and she loved to pick on the fact that I was homeschooled and didn't listen to certain music or watch certain movies or TV shows. She didn't want to come over to my house because we didn't have junk food or cable TV, and at some point I started to wonder if I was just her friend out of convenience.

When it was just the two of us hanging out or playing a game, I would often start to feel like I belonged. While the negative yet passive comments she made were embarrassing, I could get past them because I really enjoyed having a friend. But when we were around her other friends or family members who visited our church often, she shut down. I didn't get invited to her house, and we didn't play together or instant-message if anyone cooler than me was around. When it wasn't just the two of us, the only time she would talk to me was if she was talking to them about me—directly in my face.

The thing is, I knew she was a mean girl all along. But I was so desperate for a friend that I didn't care.

I chose to overlook all of it because I was so desperate to be a friend and so desperate to have a friend. I was *so* desperate that I didn't have a friend at all. I had an unstable and inconsistent person to hang around.

> One who has unreliable friends soon comes to ruin,
> but there is a friend who sticks closer than a
> brother.
>
> Proverbs 18:24

This is where my song "Games" stemmed from. The song starts off by saying,

> What's the deal with girls?
> We're friends until we're not.

So many people ask me, "What is the inspiration behind the song? What story did you hear?" or "What scenario did you witness?" The truth is, it's simply the reality that I've lived. As early as elementary school, I can think of situations with girls where I desperately tried to be a friend or to have a friend or to create a fantasy sisterhood. I saw perfect friendships in movies and I chased down the plot as if I could re-create it in real life. Ultimately, I was let down.

As I've gotten older, I've come to grips with my own insecurities and anxiousness that caused me to hope and wish and chase maybe a little too much. But I can't help but continually feel the frustration and the genuine confusion that is *mean girls*, and mean guys as well.

I know I'm not the only one who feels this way. I know I'm not the only one who's ever walked into a cafeteria weighing the options of sitting at the table where you'll be the butt of the jokes or where you may choose to compromise your integrity to laugh at someone else. I know I'm not the only one who's ever gone to college orientation hoping that your roommate will be the friend you've always wanted, or anticipating seeing the people you'll spend the next four years of your life learning with and growing with, only to feel more insecure and isolated than you did in ninth grade.

I know I'm not the only one to wonder why you weren't asked to be in a wedding when the person getting married meant the world to you. Or to wonder if you should ask someone else to be in yours because all you want is to make things right, and to show that you really are a good friend. I know I'm not the only one who has deleted and re-created and deleted and re-created again, over and over, the invitation list to a birthday party or girls' night or baby shower because you don't know who your real friends are and who they aren't. I know I'm not the only person who has reevaluated whether you should say "best friends" or "close friends" or "dear friends," or if any of those people feel like your friends at all.

There are both guys and girls who exhibit mean behavior, and there are friendships that go in and out of seasons of both flourishing and disconnect. The general action of not inviting someone to hang out, or laughing at something that wasn't intended to be a joke, doesn't make someone a bully. And when someone who used to be a close friend becomes an acquaintance, they're not automatically a mean girl, and it shouldn't be assumed that they are an enemy, as seasons do change.

However, there are those moments when you're convinced that someone will be there forever, but suddenly something beyond an accidental or awkward comment is made. It's the moment when a mean girl is born and destruction is so prevalent that you don't know if there will ever be recovery. I'm twenty-eight years old and I'm still learning how to navigate the mystery that often exists between distinguishing a friend and a foe. I know that my friends will let me down, and I am well aware that I have let them down many times. But I still battle with what is a healthy learning curve in a friendship and what is a solid line drawn between a victim and a mean girl.

Maybe you're learning how to navigate this too. Maybe there's a bully at your church, or your best friend is a bully. Maybe someone you've grown up with or someone in your own family is a bully. Maybe the fear of going to school or work or your favorite store or even your home is so significant simply because of a bully.

There are people who, for whatever reason, say or do things that tear other people apart. They make choices that offend and insult, and when you're on the other side of that choice, it can often feel as though it is completely unlikely that you will ever make a comeback.

How to Spot a Friend

We all have moments when we think negative thoughts. Someone offends us and we want to respond with words or actions that we probably shouldn't. And sometimes we may say or do something that we thought was going to be funny or enjoyable, but it turns out that someone is offended by the choice we made. When we let our words move out of our minds and turn into actions, we don't have control over who they hit and how hard. But we do have control over how we acknowledge, apologize, and seek to make amends.

I've learned that how someone behaves after they've engaged in negative language or actions can be a significant testament to their character, and even a sign as to how a person should proceed with the relationship. Specifically, when it comes to apologies, whether they realize it or not, they're oftentimes telling you if they're a genuine friend who made a mistake or a bully with no intention of changing.

External Apology

When someone hurts your feelings and their apology is focused on the external, they likely realize how their actions or words affected you. They're making the choice to focus on the impact of what they did versus the reason they did it. They're not only saying, "I'm sorry for what I did," but they're also saying

- *I understand how that affected you.*
- *I see how you were impacted.*
- *I see how that could have taken a toll on you.*

Internal Apology

When someone's apology begins and remains primarily internal, you're dealing with a selfish reaction.

- *I'm sorry I said that—I've been feeling bad.*
- *I've been in a bad mood—sorry.*

- *I'm sorry **if** there's any way you were offended by my words.*
- *It's just that this happened to me . . .* or, *It's that this person did this to me.*
- *I'm insecure, that's why I said it.*
- *You made me mad; I had no choice.*
- *I only said it because you . . .* etc.

An internal apologist is not only making excuses for their actions or justifying their words, but they're not seeing the person who was hurt. They're only seeing the offender—themselves. They likely realize there was wrongdoing, and they probably even feel some remorse or regret, but their main goal is to make sure that their name is cleared and their intentions are made known.

When you're the one hurting, it's not always easy to be concerned with someone's intentions. In that moment, the pain is so much to carry, and all you want is to be seen and heard and nothing else. External apologists focus on things outside of who they are so that their apology not only recognizes the hurt they've caused but ultimately leaves room for healing too.

Aaron and I were driving to San Diego for a mini vacation for our first wedding anniversary. We were cruising on Interstate 5, which often runs parallel to the ocean. It was an incredibly beautiful day, and it felt like we were on top of the world, heading to celebrate our small family, with the most incredible weather, in one of our favorite cities.

In an instant, everything changed.

We were driving in the far left lane when a motorcyclist sped past us, then past the car in front of us, and tried to cross in front of that car, but instead he hit the back of the vehicle two cars ahead of us. He flew off his bike and into the air, then directly into the large median. His body fell to the ground, and it felt like time had stopped.

The sound of him hitting the car was almost too much to handle.

Aaron and I screamed as he slammed on the brakes, and all I could think was, *I hope he's alive. I hope he's alive.*

The driver of the car the motorcyclist hit slammed on the brakes. The car behind that one followed suit. Within seconds, all three cars and another behind us were at a halt. Aaron and the passengers in the vehicles in front of and behind us hopped out.

In a split second, they made a choice.

They looked at the car the motorcyclist hit and saw that the woman driving seemed to be okay.

They looked at the motorcyclist lying on the ground and saw that he was unable to move.

The choice was unanimous.

Everyone rushed to the motorcyclist and gave him their full attention. The driver of the car he hit got out of her car and kneeled by the motorcyclist. He was conscious—but facing extreme injury. And she continued talking to him to make sure he stayed alert until the ambulance arrived.

I called 9-1-1. I gave them our location and a quick synopsis of what happened, making sure that I put emphasis on the motorcyclist, so they would know that, while he was alert and talking, he would need emergency help. The paramedics and fire department showed up shortly after and went to the motorcyclist. They did a quick assessment before assuring the rest of us that he would be okay and that we were free to get back in our cars and go our respective ways.

Whether we are the ones driving the car that hurts someone, or we're a random passerby, or we're even just someone called to the scene to help, we need to be intentional about serving those who are hurting.

When we apologize, we need to start with the pain we caused by our choices.

When we apologize, we need to start with the pain we caused by our choices.

It would have been very easy for that woman to say, "Well, if you hadn't switched lanes, you wouldn't have gotten hurt," or for her to begin a debate on how or if motorcyclists should travel. But in that moment, none of that mattered.

The only thing that mattered was that he was hurt. And when people around us are hurting, we need to be intentional about rushing to their side, offering care and comfort, and keeping them alert until help arrives. That is what an external apology does.

An external apology says, "I see that you're hurting. I see that you're broken. No matter who is at fault, no matter if someone was being too sensitive . . . no matter if someone was joking too much or not joking enough . . . I see you."

External apologists see beyond their intention and the starting point, and they look directly at the pain and say, "I want to mend this." And while they are likely to offend again, as all humans do, their genuine desire to understand the damage of the offense is what separates them from an internal apologist . . . a bad friend . . . a mean girl.

Searching for Closure

While I have known bullies my entire life, it is only now, in my late twenties, that I'm starting to understand the difference between these two types. I'm starting to be intentional about the boundaries I set with certain friendships and relationships, so I don't allow perpetual internal apologists into the inner circle of my life.

My goal is to be like Jesus. I'm well aware that I won't come close, but I will certainly try. Throughout the Gospels He talks about grace and forgiveness, and extending it to those around us. But for most of my life I've struggled with this, spending so much of my life reopening my heart time after time, only to get hurt again.

I fell in love with passages like Matthew 18:21–22,

> Then Peter came to Him and said, "Lord, how often shall my brother sin against me, and I forgive him? Up to seven times?" Jesus said to him, "I do not say to you, up to seven times, but up to seventy times seven" (NKJV).

This gives a somewhat tangible number as to how much to forgive. But I would often forget to scroll back to Matthew 18:15–17,

> If your brother or sister sins, go and point out their fault, just between the two of you. If they listen to you, you have won them over. But if they will not listen, take one or two others along, so that "every matter may be established by the testimony of two or three witnesses." If they still refuse to listen, tell it to the church; and if they refuse to listen even to the church, treat them as you would a pagan or a tax collector.

or ahead to Luke 17:3–4,

> So watch yourselves. "If your brother or sister sins against you, rebuke them; and if they repent, forgive them. Even if they sin against you seven times in a day and seven times come back to you saying 'I repent,' you must forgive them."

to see the importance of repentance in the equation. I would spend time becoming consumed with Jesus' incredible ability to forgive but not allow myself to really dig into the moments when Jesus encourages us to repent too.

These two things—repentance and forgiveness—go hand in hand, and Jesus, in many ways, lets us know that they're both significant. Forgiveness is important because it leads to closure and letting go of those negative moments and stepping into freedom and the future. Repentance, also important, allows us to recognize and show remorse for the choices we made. But sometimes repentance is nonexistent and we're left to try to figure out how to pick up the pieces. You may not always have the opportunity to ask a bully for an apology.

The Art of Breaking Up

Oftentimes, in searching for peace, we overanalyze what it means to have closure and anticipate finding it based on the potential vulnerability of the other person.

I remember watching a TV show in college where the main character was dating this guy that viewers really liked. They seemed like a great couple, but in true dramatic TV fashion, the writers decided they should break up. Months after their breakup (meaning a few episodes down the line), she was engaged to someone else. So she calls up her ex, invites him to dinner, and they talk about their new lives as they pursue "closure."

Though I was incredibly single at the time, I was still convinced I had some concept of how relationships worked and knew that wasn't realistic. I remember wondering why she needed to have closure with her ex, finding that a bit shady if she was supposed to be committing to the new guy. But little did I know, that's a very common thing in real life. As I talked to my peers and friends about the episode, I heard similar stories of both men and women who would meet up with people from their past in an effort to find closure.

As a married woman, I wouldn't be remotely interested in meeting up one-on-one with any guy but my husband, and I know that Aaron certainly wouldn't want to do that with an ex either. But imagine if that was the *only* way either of us could receive closure from our past? Imagine if we were dependent on the past to give us freedom to go into the future. That's saying that the past is still so present that you can't move on. That's not freedom at all. That's bondage.

I wish I had known in middle school that forgiveness doesn't require that the mean girl be my best friend. I wish I had known how to forgive her for bullying me and laughing at me in my face, and also how to say no when she invited me over to watch a movie.

I wish I had known how to extend grace to the mean girl in high school, to gracefully tell her it's not okay to laugh at the other girls at church for not having a purity ring or for cheating on a test, instead of sitting quietly because I thought grace meant being silent even when someone is doing wrong.

I wish I could have slipped myself notes and emails for my teen years and throughout my early twenties that said I could extend grace and mercy but not at the expense of inviting people into my home, into my life, and into my girls' nights.

I wish I had known that grace doesn't mean to abandon my sense of self, but instead it means to extend the most selfless act I can, as it has been extended to me.

Through the pain and the bullying I have faced in my life, I am grateful for the growth that has occurred, as my understanding of grace and truth has developed. It has allowed me to see that when others hurt me, it's often because of something significant in their lives that causes a desire to make someone else feel insignificant. Understanding this as truth and moving forward with grace, I am still as hurt as any human would be by negativity, but my recovery is much faster, and my peace is restored much sooner.

When I was around nineteen years old, I moved to a new town. I was so excited because I not only had friends in this town, but I was hopeful about the friends and music connections I could make by being in a city with my peers.

There was one girl in particular I was friends with through social media and had crossed paths with at many work events and through mutual friends. In passing, we would often exchange the common, "We've got to get together sometime!" And in my naïveté, I just *knew* that now that we lived in the same town, we would actually build a friendship.

The first time I invited her over, she texted saying she was on her way, but she never showed up. I texted her for weeks following that night and never heard back from her, but based on her activity on social media, it was obvious she had become extremely busy.

Shortly after that, I invited her out to eat with a mutual friend of ours. I told her where we were going, and she asked if I could order for her so it would be ready when she arrived. I did. Except she never showed up.

We continued to randomly cross paths around town, but never in a moment appropriate enough to mention how awkward our last "non-encounters" were. I was starting to feel ignored, neglected, and embarrassed, but ultimately I just wanted to be friends, so I tried my hardest to ignore the ever-obvious signs of a mean girl and hoped for the best.

One day I was out with friends and we ran into each other. I was immediately filled with nerves. I knew we could step to the side and have a somewhat private conversation, but I was nervous about what that could mean. But I jumped up, headed her way, and before I could say anything, she stepped aside with me and said, "I know that you've been inviting me to hang out and I know that I haven't really accepted your offer and haven't really been able to show up. But if you just keep trying—just don't give up, just keep trying. I promise, one day I'm going to show up."

I couldn't believe the words that came out of her mouth, and while I wanted to be offended, I was too busy focusing on keeping my jaw off the ground. I want to say that I responded with a quick and bewildered "Okay." But truthfully, I don't remember my response. I just remember being proud of myself for choosing to walk away.

Five years prior I would have certainly responded with "okay" and been hopeful and desperate for that relationship. I was still navigating friendship, heartache, and my place in it all, and didn't value myself enough to walk away from mean girls. But at this point in my life, I was living in a new town with a new dream, and I had a newfound confidence that allowed me to think, *She doesn't want to hang out with you*, and that was okay.

I don't have to know the reason why someone doesn't pursue a friendship with me; I just have to acknowledge that maybe she's not going to be my friend and that that's okay.

As the weeks and months progressed, for the first time in a long time, I didn't feel the pressure to text her. I didn't feel defeated as I saw her via social media hanging out with her friends. I was able to recognize the truth about her— *she doesn't want to hang out with me*—and move on. It didn't mean that she was terrible or unforgivable; it simply added grace and truth to the scenario and gave me the closure that helped me move forward.

She may be dealing with her own insecurities, struggling to balance too many friendships to add a new one, or maybe she's genuinely uninterested in me as a person, but honestly—none of that changes the way it affects me. I don't have to know the reason why someone doesn't pursue a friendship with me; I just have to acknowledge that maybe she's not going to be my friend and that that's okay.

This doesn't change my worth, it doesn't alter my value, and it doesn't mean that either of us is any less human. It simply means that I'm going to step away knowing that I am worth more than pushing, pleading, and nearly begging for connection.

It's possible you've had similar scenarios in your life that have left you wondering where you stand with someone.

Why didn't I get invited?
Why am I not in the group text?
Why wasn't I a bridesmaid?
Why wasn't I invited to the baby shower?
Why didn't I get to go on the camping trip?
Why don't I get invited to the movies?

I don't know the exact reasons why people do or don't do certain things, but I do know that when we allow our worth and our value to be defined by who we are and *Whose* we are instead of what other people think about us, we can begin to walk in freedom.

There were times, before the awkward restaurant encounter, when I was truly heartbroken and nearly bitter. If she came up in conversation, I felt the need to change the subject or just get on my phone to distract myself from the feelings of inadequacy. But now, even when I see her in person, I am able to offer a "Hey, hope you're well!" with no expectation of friendship and no bitterness to follow.

True friend. 10.8.19.

I thought she was a true friend.

The stand up, stick it out, real talk true friend.
The fly across the country for a visit kind of a real friend,
plan a road trip, I pay the bill, you take the tip true
friend.

I thought she was a true friend.

And I thought I was a true friend.

The two of us matched like a new kind of sisterhood I'll be
Amber you be Alexis God bless America, keep it lively in
the neighborhood a true friend.

But sometimes even the real ones.

Sometimes even the day ones.

The ones you thought you could trust put the car in
reverse and before you could fight the temptation to
curse you're a VW beetle with no one to believe in.

Your closest companion has switched up the gears and
traded you in for her new dreams the sequel.

You're the original version, the start to the story, but
this novel is over and you take no glory—after gossip
and rumors and texts and DMs and drama that you
thought you were too old to get in but you're here.

She's there.

At the other end of a table and you don't have a chair.
A seat. A place. Anywhere to belong. You're all by
yourself. There's no way to right these wrongs.

You're searching for closure, hoping for freedom but all
that you find is anger and disbelief—

Because you thought she was a true friend.

FINDING QUIET

Mean girls and bullies may not ever go away. I thought such problems would end in middle or even high school, but I've graduated from college, only have a few years left of my twenties, have a full-time job, and can say that these situations continue to show up. But it's up to us how we react, and it's up to us how we choose to value ourselves, regardless of what anyone else's actions or words say about us.

If you ever have a moment when you don't get invited somewhere or you feel isolated at a table alone while everyone else seems to be having a good time, I want to challenge you to do the most unnatural thing in that moment: **embrace it**.

Don't get me wrong, I have been the kid, teen, *and* adult hoping for an invitation to the table or the party—and it's hard. You feel alone, embarrassed, and insecure, and oftentimes you start to feel insecure and embarrassed about the fact that you *are* insecure and embarrassed! I don't want to downplay friendlessness, but together we're going to choose to see those moments as a state of **quiet** instead of loneliness.

So next time you find yourself in the quiet, while everyone else is enjoying the noise, I want you to say to yourself, *They don't want to hang out with me*, and immediately after, I want you to welcome the quiet and **listen** for whatever it is God may be wanting to show you in that exact moment.

I have had many moments like this, and these are some of the things God has shown me when I've welcomed the quiet:

1. You are more than what others think about you.
2. She is treating you this way because of her own brokenness. Don't allow her pain to cause you so much pain that you choose to hurt others too.
3. I will cover you. I will protect you. You do not need to fight this fight.

4. You are rushing to do more, be more, and have more, when right now I want you to learn to enjoy time with Me, even if you don't have anything else.

5. There is someone across the room who is also sitting alone. If you make the choice to be the friend you need to them, you will not only bless someone else, but you will be blessed in the process.

This is only a glimpse of what I have learned in the quiet. What do you think God might be wanting to teach you?

ten

Tempted to Compare

I used to tell people that my sister and I were twins. Morgan was almost two years older—twenty-one months, to be exact—but she was my best friend, and I wanted to be as close to her as possible, so being twins seemed to be the solution. While I knew that we couldn't just "be twins," I was often frustrated by that fact.

Because we were so close in age and height, our mom used to put a lot of emphasis on making sure that we were different. She would oftentimes coordinate our outfits, or even dress us alike, but she would also remind us that we were individuals. She wanted us to know that it was okay for us to be best friends but also have our own lives. There were times my sister would get invited somewhere, and my mom would say to me, "That seems like something that's more suited for your sister and her friends. Why don't we go do this instead?" At first I would get jealous, but I eventually realized that my mom was helping me to find my own identity.

Morgan discovered her passion and talent for art at a young age. While I would draw as a hobby, my mom never pushed me into it, knowing that it was not only not a passion of mine, but it wasn't one of my strengths. Her philosophy in raising us partnered with my sister's consistent answer "No" to my persistent request to be my twin, resulting in my developing a healthy perspective on learning to appreciate who I was, appreciate the good in others, and not compare the two.

However, the world still found it seemingly necessary to compare us on a regular basis. I was about nine when an adult that I trusted said to me—for no reason—"Wow, your sister has much longer hair than you do!" It had never bothered me that my sister's hair was longer. But in that moment, I started to wonder if that was better, if my hair wasn't good because it wasn't as long. I think she read all of that in my reaction as she quickly responded with, "But it's okay! Because you have lighter eyes."

That was the first time I learned that people praise lighter eyes and longer hair. In just two sentences, this woman taught me more about insecurities and comparison than I had learned in nearly ten years of living. While I'm grateful that my mom later helped me understand the root of those issues, those comments opened up a door for constant conversation about comparison.

People love to pit people against each other, especially women, and especially sisters.

Morgan and I frequently share the stage together, whether

speaking, singing, or a mixture of both. We've been told that I talk too much and should give Morgan more of the spotlight, when in reality, Morgan typically asks me to take more of the lead because she knows my strengths. With our dynamic, she feels more comfortable helping to plan and orchestrate what will be said, then giving me the space to bring those words to the surface.

While the world is comparing us, we are championing each other, and it is up to us to make sure that we silence the voices of negativity.

Morgan is known for sharing quotes and poetry on social media. Some people may look at my page and see the occasional quote-style post and start to compare me to my sister, saying, "Oh, you're trying to be like your sister." But the truth is, any quote I put on social media that is beautifully designed was designed by my sister, and I posted it because she encouraged me to do so. One of her strengths is encouraging others and helping to create for others, and I'm so grateful that she cares about me enough to help me in that way.

Sometimes it feels like my sister and I don't always have the chance to celebrate each other because the world is sitting and waiting to hear how we stack up to one another. We don't care which one of us is charting on the radio or has more Instagram followers, or even who makes more money or more accolades. While the world is comparing us, we are championing each other, and it is up to us to make sure that we silence the voices of negativity.

Slipping into Comparison

Right before I found out that I was pregnant with my daughter, I knew I wanted to make some changes with my health. I wasn't incredibly satisfied with my gym routine, and I was at a crossroads because I really wasn't sure if I wanted to work on losing weight or try something new and athletic that would build muscle, or maybe even a bit of both.

When I became pregnant, I decided it wasn't the best timing to pursue a brand-new athletic adventure, so I decided to wait until after I had the baby. When Isabella was only a few weeks old, I remember seeing an actress on TV who was about my age. She was also about my height and my complexion, and our hair was even about the same length. She had a really cool personality, and I immediately thought, *Wow, she's so cool. I want to follow her on Instagram.*

I was really inspired by her posts about body positivity and confidence, and I even started to take some notes about her health choices, as I knew they could inspire my own. Every time I would see her on social media, I was motivated to try something new in the gym or to work harder on setting and achieving goals.

But unfortunately, that joy and energy didn't last very long.

What started out as my seeing one of her posts and thinking, *Wow, she's awesome*, soon became *Wow, I wish I was awesome.*

And gradually turned into *Wow, I will never be like that.*

I followed her with the intention of being inspired, but ended up feeling defeated. I knew that I was not secure enough in my own identity, so I eventually chose to unfollow her.

Surprisingly, once I unfollowed her, I didn't feel an immediate relief from pressure to be like someone else. But *she* wasn't actually the issue. I was. It was a wise choice not to spend all day swiping through social media, especially seeing her posts, but ultimately I had to do the work myself to find my value in who *I* am and who I *could* be.

Comparison is crippling. What can start off as innocent admiration can quickly and easily turn into self-destruction. We can trick ourselves into believing that we're taking notes or being inspired, but really we're just making an even longer list of the things we don't like about ourselves.

It's possible to admire someone and to be inspired by someone without allowing yourself to continually compare yourself to that person. But when you start to neglect who you are in order to invest in who they've worked hard to become, you've begun to tread the waters of comparison.

What We Should (and Shouldn't) Compare

I love online shopping. As much as I love people, stores stress me out. And I have a really difficult time making decisions, so I'm pretty sure sales associates are stressed out by me. I don't take fifteen to twenty minutes to decide on a purchase—I need hours, if not days or weeks.

Tabs are always open on my computer. I always have way too many tabs open, most of which are websites that sell music or video production gear. Within those tabs are worlds full of pages comparing the differences between three or four pieces of recording equipment. I spend days looking at all the different features laid out to see which one is the best bang for my buck. Sometimes I'm not even making a purchase; I'm just so fascinated by gear that I want to know what new products are on the market.

There are few places in life that offer the proper context for comparison.

- Your Amazon cart that you just won't press "Buy" in because you're watching YouTube videos comparing similar products or trying to see if you can get cheaper shipping elsewhere.
- That activity in magazines where you're trying to figure out what is different between Picture A and Picture B.
- Standing in the grocery store, trying to figure out if you should buy the name-brand box of pasta or the store brand that's a little bit cheaper. It might be shaped differently and have no visible logo, but you're positive the flavor will still be exactly what you want.

Those are the appropriate times for comparison.

When you can't make a decision, you get stuck in a comparison loop. You start going back and forth, trying to figure out which one is best. We find ourselves pressing "Save for later" in our online shopping carts, and sometimes even forgoing the box of pasta entirely because we couldn't decide which one we liked better.

This is why it is *imperative* that we decide who we are.

When we *don't* know who we are, we start going back and forth, as though we are a product that can be purchased or a potential investment to be made. We look at people around us and begin a cycle of picking and choosing desirable elements of who they are, instead of embracing every element of who we are.

We mindlessly swipe through social media and see a family that seems to have it all together in a way our family doesn't, and we sit there comparing ourselves to them, instead of spending time with our *real* family in *real* time and in *real* life.

Comparison is the foundation of destruction, and the irony of that is not lost. Picking and choosing from other people's lives could seem like we are creating a dream life for ourselves, but what we're really doing is creating the basis on which our lives will fall apart, because we no longer have the parts of who *we* are. We are only fragments of other people.

When the impulse to compare finds its way to us, I have noticed that there are two ways it displays itself. *External comparisons* are the things that are said by us or to us that blatantly compare us to another person or their abilities or success. The words can be painful or subtle or passive-aggressive.

Internal comparisons are the feelings and thoughts we experience, often subconsciously, that may never be spoken aloud but can be the starting point for ruminating on negative things.

And then there's the weird mix—a little bit internal, a little bit external—like a terribly mixed homemade lemonade when you can feel the gritty sugar going through your teeth with every sip. It's all a part of this weird human experience of trying to manage what others say and think about us plus what we think of ourselves. It may start out as a thought or even a comment, but before we know it, something we heard in passing or said in our heads can spiral into jealousy, hardening our heart toward someone else, and even leading to resentment.

Examples of external comparisons are

- The things people say to us that draw a comparison between us and our siblings, peers, co-workers, cousins, etc.
- The way media often encourages us to compare our physical features to other women (and men) with commercials, online ads, and magazine headlines, e.g., "Do *you* want flawless skin?"
- The commentary we make when we go to a friend's house and see that their car is cleaner than ours, which we try to pass off as a joke but is really a negative comment about what we *don't* have when we could have just made a positive comment about what they *do* have.
- The moments we say "You are goals!" or comment "#couplegoals" in response to a social media post by someone we wish we could be like.

And then there are internal comparisons:

- The feeling of disappointment in our own wardrobe when we see the way our friends or models on social media are dressed.
- The discouragement we experience when seeing bigger or better houses that belong to people we know, or even celebrities or influencers in online "house tour" videos.

- The negative thoughts we have about ourselves when we see someone living out our dream career.
- The choice to leave the gym, or not go, because of the thought of not looking like someone else.

Whether external, internal, or a weird mix of both, all comparison is detrimental in the end. Personally, I find internal comparison to be much sneakier and much harder to recognize. When we're comparing externally, it's not only easier to catch ourselves, but other people may notice it sooner too.

When we spend time feeling insecure because we're not like someone else, we begin to doubt every aspect of who we are. Before we know it, we've not only lost a sense of feeling satisfied with how we look or the life we live, but we start to genuinely lose sight of our purpose in life.

But it doesn't have to be this way.

There is something beautiful that happens when we are confident enough in who we are to be able to look at someone else and admire who *they* are. We should be able to say to someone, "I love your hair," or "Your family is beautiful," without having the thought that our hair is not beautiful or our family is not good enough. But when we start to want what they have, instead of wanting who we already are, we have entered into a world of comparison that is far from what God wants for us.

We are more than the online shopping carts and music production comparison charts. We are more than the choice between the four-bedroom with less square footage or the three-bedroom with the dream kitchen. We are more than

Option 1 vs. Option 2 or finding the difference between pictures A and B.

Individually we are fearfully and wonderfully made. And we deserve to step into the purpose and the calling made for each of us, and *not* worry or wonder if we match up to anyone else.

I have to learn to be okay with who I am—and the more I decide that only *I* can be who *I* was made to be, the more I will find that I cannot be compared with anyone.

You have to learn to be okay with who you are too—and the more you decide that only *you* can be who *you* were made to be, the more you will find that you cannot be compared with anyone.

Sometimes, we can learn this lesson by embracing the relationships that God has put in our lives. Whether I'm comparing myself against someone else or against a version of myself that I wish I could be, I can find myself in a downward spiral of self-deprecating thoughts that cause anxiety, panic, and sometimes even periods of full shutdown.

As I was single until I met Aaron, I spent most of my twenties living alone and learning to cope with shutting down by myself. I would also like to point out that "learning to cope" sometimes meant shutting down and waiting it out in the silence—not the good silence, though. The sad silence that needs to be broken. So basically, there were times when I wasn't coping at all.

Morgan recently released a book titled *All Along You Were Blooming*. It's a beautiful compilation of her artwork and poetry that not only tells stories but has genuinely changed lives. On the day of a major book-signing event in Los Angeles, I started ruminating on my negative thoughts, and I found myself sitting on the floor and staring at the wall, emotionally afraid to move. I began experiencing irrational fears about why I shouldn't attend her event, and then started to have anxiety about what people would think of me if I wasn't there. Before I knew it, I was thinking every negative thought about who I was, and convincing myself that everything would be better off without me.

I wish I could tell you that as a follower of Christ I don't have these moments. I wish it were realistic to say that because I'm writing this book, I have everything figured out. But I don't. I have moments when I lose sight of who I am, of Whose I am, and I feel myself falling apart.

As I sat there in my pain and self-doubt, my husband came and knelt in front of me. Aaron's an amazing husband, but he's also my best friend. And he began talking me through the reasons why I *should* attend my sister's event, and how upset I would be if I didn't go.

If you have ever had an emotional break like this, then you know that the last thing you may want is someone speaking truth into your life. It's in those moments that it's easier to push away the people we love, and speak negativity toward every ounce of hope they try to share. And I did. Because I'm really good at it. But my best friend is equally good, if not better, at acknowledging my worth, my value, and pouring it right back into me.

Our friends and family members are not the source of our hope, worth, or value, but they are reminders of those things in the moments we are too weak to embrace them for ourselves. When we begin to lack self-esteem and we put ourselves down for not being good enough or strong enough, they see what we can't see, and they help us press on.

We have to be intentional and wise about who we allow in our lives and choose to embrace when God is speaking through them. We cannot allow the pain and heaviness of our present to outweigh the significance of what God says about our future. And *He* says that He has a plan and a purpose for our lives.

The key to fighting the urge to compare ourselves with other people is finding a sense of purpose that cannot be lived out by anyone else. Because it's one thing to know who God says you are, but it's another thing to walk it out and live it out.

We cannot allow the pain and heaviness of our present to outweigh the significance of what God says about our future.

I didn't feel like living out my purpose that night. I wanted to walk in the bondage of insecurity that seemed to feel easier in the moment (while simultaneously heavier—am I right? Yeah). I wanted to allow my character complexities to trigger my neurological differences and send me down a road I knew would only hurt me in the end. But my friend, my husband, wouldn't let me. He saw me how God sees me, and while it took tears and quite a bit of time out of our afternoon, he helped me accept it too. The rest of our day was spent listening to worship music and a podcast on creativity, and getting drive-through tacos on our four-hour round-trip drive to Los Angeles to attend my sister's event.

Once there, we not only had a great time supporting my sister and connecting with family and friends, but we were approached by a couple with a similar story to ours, who asked us how to balance emotional complexities in their relationship. And as we talked to them, it was like a light bulb went off. Whether I *feel* like I can walk in my purpose or not, God is always setting the path for me to do so. Whether I *feel* confident in who I am or not, God is always ready to use me. Whether I *feel* proud of who He made me to be or not, He is writing a story that is worth being told, and He wants me to be able to trust Him enough to share it.

FINDING QUIET

Turn off all music, set all distractions aside, and take a few moments in the quiet to do one of these things:

1. **Write your name as beautifully as you can.**

    There's a cliché that when a girl has a crush on a guy, she starts to write her name (followed by his last name!) in cursive or a fun print all over a notebook. I can neither confirm nor deny that I know what this is like by personal experience, but I do know that more than imagining who you *could* be, there is freedom in embracing who you *are.*

    Get a journal, some random paper, or even this book and **write your name as beautifully as you can** and as many times as possible until you start to smile. Write your name until you begin to embrace that it's who you are. Write your name until you say it out loud with confidence, knowing that no one else can even *try* to be who you are or fulfill the purpose destined for your life.

2. Embrace your uniqueness.

Journal or say aloud the things that make you feel insecure or that tempt you to compare yourself with others. Then write or say at least three things that are *positive* about each thing on your list.

If you're having a challenging time finding something positive, ask a close friend or family member; often, the things we consider weaknesses in ourselves are the things that draw people to us. I used to feel insecure about being goofy, talking too much, and simply not fitting in with the cool kids. Little did I know that my career would be built around needing a lot of words, humor, and reliability that certainly couldn't be found in being "cool."

There are things about your insecurities that give you a perspective and a view on life that you wouldn't have otherwise. So take some time, be honest, and begin to **embrace your uniqueness.**

3. Set long-term goals for yourself, and short-term goals to match.

Sometimes we compare ourselves with other people because there are things about who we are that we want to change. However, the solution is *not* to allow another person to be the standard for our own success. Only *we* can determine who we want to be and how much we're willing to invest to get there.

When discovering what that means for us individually, it's important that we **set long-term goals *and* short-term goals to match.**

Long-term goals are those that will not likely happen right away. Setting a long-term goal allows us to see down the line three to six months, nine to twelve months, or even a few years:

- I want to get my degree.
- I want to quit my nine-to-five and work full time from home.
- I want to lose one hundred pounds.
- I want to buy a house.
- I want to try to succeed at a new sport.

Short-term goals are those that can be achieved within a month, weeks, or even *a day*. It's important to set short-term goals that match your long-term goals so that you don't become discouraged along the way.

- I will study for my classes five hours each day.
- I will save 5 percent of every paycheck to invest in my business.
- I will work out five days a week.
- I will meet with a real estate agent this week.
- I will sign up for a new sport this month and see what it's like.

Write down both your long- and short-term goals, and place them on your bathroom counter, nightstand—anywhere you'll see them every day. So when you're tempted to compare yourself with someone else, you have a reference point: who *you* are/want to be versus where someone else currently is.

eleven

Pondering Purpose

You may want to say it out loud, journal it, or simply think through this question and your answer, but I want you to ask yourself:

What am I fighting for?

In my mid-twenties, I became fascinated with boxing. As the granddaughter of a former semi-pro boxer (my maternal grandfather) and a boxing hobbyist (paternal grandfather), I've always found it to be intriguing, but I personally thought that the idea of hitting someone else—or getting hit—was terrifying.

Somewhere around my twenty-fifth summer, I realized that boxing gyms afford the opportunity to learn the technique and strategy without actually boxing another person. I learned the term *sparring*, which means I could train like a boxer and never actually step into a ring with the expectation that one person would leave the ring as a winner and the other—not so much.

I was hooked.

I joined a local boxing gym and found myself going there more than any other gym I had joined. My paternal grandfather, Papa, passed away when I was in college, but I know that if the reaction of my granddaddy (my maternal grandfather) was any indication, he would be immensely proud.

Even though I love boxing (so much so that I became certified to teach even though I've never taught a class; I'm just a nerd who wanted to learn more, and that seemed the best way), I still get nervous during any kind of fight scene in a movie. I know that it's so obviously choreographed, but physical contact makes me uneasy! Even so, I recently went to the movies with my family to watch a popular film about a boxer—and I loved it.

There was one scene in particular where a fighter in the film, who longed to make his family proud of him, was at the top of his game—well, fight. Throughout the film we learn about his disconnect with family—particularly his mom—and in many ways you could say that he just wanted to earn her affection and love. In this particular fight, his mom showed up and, as he's winning, his pride was at an all-time high.

Then she walks out. She's no longer watching him fight, and you can see his physical shift and feel his emotional adjustments when he realizes that his mom no longer cares. All of a sudden, *he* no longer cares, because he wasn't fighting for himself. He wasn't fighting for his own purpose; he was fighting to prove something to someone else. So once she was out of the room, he lost all sense of why he was even in the ring.

And he lost.

What are you fighting for?

Who are you fighting for?

It's All about the Why

It may seem dramatic to ask yourself questions about fighting if you have little to no interest in boxing in general—or if you're like me and you like punching a bag or training with a coach but you don't ever want to actually *fight* someone. But the thing is, every day of our lives is a fight, though it isn't a physical battle, as Ephesians 6:12 says:

> For our struggle is not against flesh and blood, but against the rulers, against the authorities, against the powers of this dark world and against the spiritual forces of evil in the heavenly realms.

Every day that we wake up, we are faced with the choice of pursuing our calling and our purpose, or giving in to doubt, negativity, and the schemes that are against the very thing we should be living for. We have to choose between chasing good or bad, dark or light, things that are evil or things that are heavenly.

What are you fighting for?
Who are you fighting for?

> *Every day . . . we are faced with the choice of pursuing our calling and our purpose, or giving in to doubt, negativity, and the schemes that are against the very thing we should be living for.*

Aaron and I are both former teachers. He was full time in a traditional daycare setting, and I led my church's children's ministry. As we desire to be either a homeschool family or very involved in our children's traditional school environment, we have frequent conversations about education.

One common strategy—often in grade school—that we don't particularly endorse is the practice some teachers use to bring the students' focus back to them. In a classroom of twenty children, if only five are paying attention when it is time for class to begin, some teachers will call out individual children's behavior in an effort to encourage the remaining fifteen children to prepare for class.

Johnny is paying attention!
Wow, Sarah is doing a great job listening.
Davis knows how to listen. Good job!

I'm not here for it. At all.

I fully support encouraging children when they are doing the right thing. As a parent, as a mentor, as someone whose degree is in child and youth development and children's ministry, I have seen firsthand the results that come from positive reinforcement, and I am all about it! But what I *don't* like is using one child's behavior as the driving force for another child.

I don't want my daughter to be in any environment where she feels compelled to do what she is supposed to do only because someone else is doing it. I want her to be able to hear "It's time to pay attention" from a trusted adult and *want* to pay attention, instead of choosing to do it because Johnny did it first.

I want Isabella to have a sense of purpose whether someone else is watching or not. I want her to be driven to do what she is called to do without needing to know if someone else is doing it.

We want to raise our daughter to know her *why*, and we *don't* want it to be dependent on someone else.

When I was diagnosed with Tourette Syndrome, I was told I would probably never go to college. At that time, kids with Tourette's were not given much hope to have a normal life— certainly not a thriving one. It was expected that we would never gain independence or freedom due to the condition's severity or the medication's effects.

When I *did* go to college, when I got a good grade on a paper or was accepted into the position I wanted in a certain group or club, I had to remind myself *why* I was there. There were so many times when I wanted to call the doctors who said I would never accomplish certain goals and say, "See! I did it. You were wrong!" While they were **so** wrong and I **did** reach my goals, I chose to fight against the urge to become filled with pride for proving them wrong, because I didn't go to college to prove anyone wrong. My *why* was founded in pursuing a degree in something I loved.

When our *why* is not focused on our own purpose but rather on other people, we begin to feel lost when those people are no longer in the picture. When we go to college or choose a career to prove someone wrong (or right), what happens when that person isn't at graduation? Or doesn't show interest in our life anymore? And when we teach our children to behave because their siblings or classmates are doing it, what happens when their siblings and classmates aren't there?

If our daily fight is to prove something to other people, it's never going to be worth it. It's never going to be enough.

We will spend every day hoping and wishing that the mom in the crowd or the "haters" from the internet would see our every move and finally believe in us. But what happens when they don't?

We need to know why we do what we do and why we are who we are, because if we're just living for other people, then we are living in constant comparison. We're parading around the consistent feeling that we have to be at the top of our game, and sometimes the top of everybody else's game, *just* to be somebody. Just to be something.

What are you fighting for?

We have to think about these things when we're trying out for a new team or touring a home with a real estate agent. We have to ask ourselves these questions when we're swiping through Instagram or applying for a new job. We have to look inside ourselves when we feel we're too anxious and eager to find out who is DMing us or who wants to get coffee with us.

Because there will come a time when we can't distinguish the voices of everyone around us. There will come a time when no one else's opinions or thoughts can be heard or read.

We will find ourselves in the quiet places with the choices we've made, and we will have to decide what we are living for, what our life is really about.

A lot of my peers have made the decision, sometimes more than once, to do a social media cleanse. I have definitely done this before, and when it was over, I knew that I had made the right decision. For me, it was just after I had gotten married, and for the first time in my life, there was always someone in my room. Ha! I started to realize how much I enjoyed binge-watching a Netflix series *with* someone, and the constant of having my best friend around, and I neglected social media without even realizing it.

It turned into an intentional cleanse when I realized how much more fun life moments were when I wasn't worried about how I would recap them into a photo and a caption. I wasn't enjoying time as half of a brand-new duo thinking, *This would be a great vlog!* Granted, creating content *is* a part of my job, and I genuinely love it, but everyone needs a break from both hobbies and work, and I'm grateful I took that time.

Ultimately, I believe that people do a social media cleanse to figure out who they are and what they want aside from the likes, the attention, and the instant gratification it can bring.

But here's the thing: As awesome as a social media cleanse can be, social media is not the root of the issue.

If the issue with social media is that we're looking for validation from other people, taking the smartphone away is not going to come close to solving that problem. Because the second you're walking through the mall . . . the second you're in the gym . . . the second someone new starts working at your job who makes you feel insecure about your image or your talents, those same feelings of being invalid will show up again.

We have to be able to step back and ask ourselves, Why am I here? What am I living for? What am I fighting for?

Feeling a lack of purpose is a fundamental issue that has to be addressed, whether we have smartphones or not. We have to be able to step back and ask ourselves, *Why am I here? What am I living for?* **What am I fighting for?**

I'm so grateful that at an early age I became pretty invested in my faith. That's not to say that I have not had struggles and complexities. But my faith has been my greatest help in the moments when I've lost sight of my value or worth.

What am I fighting for?

Because of my faith, I am confident in my answer.

Finding My Purpose

I was single for much longer than I've been married. And when I was single, there was a certain part of my job that was harder than anything else. I have always loved being onstage. It's exciting when hundreds or even thousands of people are singing along and having a good time.

In the early days of my career, I had moments when being onstage was where I felt the most confident. I felt important and like I mattered, and when I walked offstage to go sign autographs, I felt as though people cared about me and liked me.

Those experiences were amazing—and they still are! They're not the source of my hope or joy, but I can truly say that starting out as a full-time artist, I *did* find my hope in the loud moments of feeling loved and appreciated.

But then I would get in the car or the tour bus and go to the hotel. My ears would still be ringing from all of the noise, so I would shower with no music playing, or even a podcast, and then I would sit, with no makeup on and my hair all over the place, in sweatpants, alone. I would be in a hotel room by myself in absolute silence.

By the time I get off work it's usually one or two o'clock in the morning. Most of my friends are asleep, soon to be getting ready for their normal jobs. And while I know I could call my parents anytime, they're still not going to be on the phone with me 24/7. In those moments, it was just me. And the quiet.

I want to make sure that I note that in my singlehood, and even now, the idea of messy hair, sweatpants, and a quiet room after a productive and enjoyable evening at work sounds incredible. And one of my favorite things about my husband is that he loves date nights with sweatpants and pizza just as much as I do. There's nothing wrong with a quieter evening. It's actually beautiful. But the issue is when the noise is put on a pedestal, and the quiet begins to feel like a downgrade.

What are you fighting for?
What is your purpose?

When I was too captivated by crowds, my answer would have been "people." I was beginning to find my purpose in bringing joy to other people's lives. And when I was in a quiet room and couldn't see that joy on people's faces, I felt like I had lost my sense of purpose.

I had to start being intentional about focusing on the answer to the question, "Jamie Grace, what are you fighting for? What is your purpose?"

I started to realize that it wasn't my purpose to bring people joy. Instead, it was my purpose to live a life full of God's joy, in hopes of directing people to the Source.

If life were a screenplay we're the director. God is the Source —the Writer. He speaks first, *then* we can work. Navigating through every day, bringing His message to life as we tell the stories He's written. Then He follows through as the Editor and Producer, correcting us along the way and making the final calls about every moment, as He has the final say.

It wasn't my purpose to bring people joy. Instead, it was my purpose to live a life full of God's joy, in hopes of directing people to the Source.

There's a significant difference in living a life to give to others and living a life that directs people to the One who is the greatest at giving all things. Our goal should be to direct. Not to create. Because there is a Creator available to all of us, who creates in a way much greater than we ever could. And when He gives us the privilege to be a part of those designs, we know that we have found our purpose.

What are you fighting for?

The more I surround myself with the real answer to that question, the less those quiet moments have a negative effect on me. I still have an *incredible* time onstage and signing autographs, and I hope I get to have this job for a really long time! But now when I step away from the sound and the lights, I know that my purpose remains—I haven't left it on the stage.

There is so much joy in performing in a coffee shop, a church, a theater, or even an arena. But please, take no offense to this if you've ever been in the audience—my purpose can't be for the crowd. Because when they are gone, what am I living for then? I had to learn that my purpose in the arena had to be the same as my purpose outside of the arena, so that once I left it, I still had joy and felt complete.

How to Find Your Why

So how do you find that purpose? I could be used in direct-ing people to God's joy whether I am a singer or a teacher or a stay-at-home mom. So how do *you* discover what it is that you've been called to do?

Here's a series of questions to journal, ponder, or even ask yourself out loud.

1. Where has God placed you?

What's your arena? Where do you spend most of your time? Where is the place you feel the most validated? The most complete? The most full?

- If you're an athlete, your arena might be on the court or field where you play.
- If you're a teacher, your arena might be in the classroom.
- If you're a pastor, it's likely when you're with your congregation.
- If you're a college student, your arena might be your dorm room or the cafeteria.
- If you're a wife, husband, or parent, it's likely when you're home with your family.
- If you're an artist or actor, social media might be your arena.

Wherever you spend your time is your arena. Wher-ever you speak your heart and have the privilege of an audience—whether an audience of one or a million—*that* is where God is using you to fulfill your purpose.

2. What is God putting on your heart?

So, what is your purpose while you're in your arena?

While I love that question, I like to tackle it from the other end of the spectrum and ask, What makes you upset about your environment? What is the thing that happens in your arena that you wish you could change? What do you want to be different about your arena or about arenas that are similar to yours?

- If you're an athlete, you might hope for a more positive environment within your team or league.

- If you're a teacher, you may desire for your co-workers to feel more appreciated or for your students to be filled with motivation or drive.

- If you're a pastor, there may be times when you want to see more action led by compassion within your congregation or ministry partners.

- If you're a college student, you might want more rest! Or understanding.

- If you're a wife, husband, or parent, you might hope for more structure, gratitude, grace.

- If you're an artist or actor, you may hope for more art to be created for reasons other than for profit.

The things that keep us returning to our knees asking God *Why? When?* and *How?* are not mindless burdens meant to be ignored. They are often the very issues put on our hearts so that *we* can be a part of directing those around us to a solution.

The solution to that problem is your purpose.

3. How will you allow God to use you?

How can God use that purpose when I'm outside of the arena? How can my purpose become a daily walk that exists outside of where I spend most of my time?

You may go through seasons of different jobs, careers, or living in different cities or even different countries. Your friend groups may change, your family dynamics may shift, but when you see a lack of peace, and God places you in the room where it's needed, He is calling you to be the one to direct the room to a place of peace.

- When God places you in a situation that seems hopeless, He may very well be using you to remind others of His hope.

- When God calls you to a place of negativity and doubt, He may be calling you to tell of His goodness and mercy.

- When God's grace carries you through a friendship that brings hurt and pain, He may be calling you to extend the same grace you've received, whether the friendship lasts or not.

God is calling us daily to direct our friends, family members, peers, and everyone around us to Him and His faithfulness and love. When we not only accept the call but also surround ourselves with people who are stepping into this calling, we are promised a fulfilling life. What more could we ask for?

I am the gate; whoever enters through me will be saved. They will come in and go out, and find pasture. The thief comes only to steal and kill and destroy; I have come that they may have life, and have it to the full. I am the good shepherd. The good shepherd lays down his life for the sheep."

John 10:9–11

Then there comes a time when you step off social media, when you step out of the classroom, when you leave the church. There comes a time when you step out of the arena and it's just you and the quiet.

These are the moments when we can choose to *still* embrace purpose. When we can still accept the call to be a representation of faithfulness, love, peace, joy, and hope whether someone is around or not. Whether people hear us, see us, or notice us. We can still choose to live a life of purpose.

How I Found My Why

1. Where is my arena?

I remember standing next to my mom and helping her lead worship for our church of fewer than thirty people. I was about six or seven years old and I loved singing. I was having fun, but it had nothing to do with holding a microphone or how my voice sounded. I saw the looks on people's faces as they connected with the words they were singing, and I realized that music was a direct line to feelings. I knew that no matter what I did in life and no matter where I ended up, I was supposed to be a part of bringing those words, those feelings, to people.

2. What is God putting on my heart?

*What is the thing that happens in the arena that I wish
I could change?*

As I got older and continually found myself revisiting
Psalm 30:5, I *knew* I was discovering what I wanted to
embrace and change.

For his anger lasts only a moment,\
    but his favor lasts a lifetime;
weeping may stay for the night,
    but rejoicing comes in the morning.

Psalm 30:5

How could a verse speak of **anger** *and* **favor?** How
could both **weeping** *and* **rejoicing** exist in the short span
of just one night and morning? And how could I find a
way to share them both?

God would oftentimes put people in my life who were
overwhelmed by the pressure to rush their grief so they
could arrive at a perfect peace. They felt as though they
couldn't experience joy because they were too caught up
in pain. I was one of those people. And God spoke to me,
allowing me to experience Him fully even in my imper-
fections. As I realized that there were so many other kids,
teens, moms, and dads—literally every kind of human
existing in the world—who were trying to find a Psalm
30:5 voice, I knew that I had to spend my life singing
with mine as loud as I could.

3. How will you allow God to use you?

Wherever you choose, God. Just use me.

This is my prayer. For the concerts where the tickets are purchased at a rate that makes a concert promoter proud. For the social media posts I share that don't get much engagement with the exception of the few people who really need to see them. For the friends I have had since I was young, and the onetime conversations I have with people in the grocery store. I constantly ask God to soften my heart to the broken, to help me navigate how to meet them where they are, and to bring them joy if it's what He would have me do.

Most people don't believe me when I tell them that I'm an introvert. I can talk for as many hours as my lungs will allow, and even if I start to lose my breath, there's no need to worry because I always carry my inhaler with me. But when it comes to needing a moment to recharge and get ready to face the world, I crave alone time. I would rather stay home than go anywhere, and I don't understand why most physical stores exist when clearly online shopping is literally a gift.

I recharge alone, or in near-quiet moments with my family, but once my battery is full, I'm ready to *go.* And *when* I'm ready to go, whether I'm standing in line at the DMV (musician life— I've moved a *lot*, y'all), sitting in a waiting room, or honestly if I just see a human with a cool hairstyle, I am ready to talk. I have to remind myself not to ask too many questions or talk too fast because all I can think about are the things that we go through as people and the joy that we have access to as children of God.

Unless I was sick or the travel arrangements or the

venue booking was out of my control, I have always signed autographs at the end of my concerts. I've always thought it was a bit silly that people wanted my autograph, to the point that on my first official tour when I was seventeen, I didn't realize that I hadn't come up with an autograph until the line after the show had begun. So I dug into my homeschool skills and wrote my name in cursive, but all lowercase—because I'm a rebel. More than ten years later, that's still my signature.

Interestingly enough, I soon realized that as much as I love singing and being an "entertainer," I liked the "signing line" much more. Being onstage gave me the chance to share my words and my melodies, but the signing line was the other half of the conversation. Connecting with people as equals, exchanging thoughts, was much more significant than the singular direction of artist to listener.

It's during that signing time that I have heard testimonies: single women who hear my music and learn that it's okay to be single and content while also desiring to get married someday; kids with Tourette Syndrome who are frustrated by their tics and medication but are proud to be unique; parents whose families are battling crises from financial to finding a church home, yet they spent the evening rejoicing in the goodness of God—and I get to celebrate the goodness with them.

It is my goal . . . my dream . . . my hope . . . my purpose that these conversations continue to happen onstage, in songs, in autograph lines, in my home, with my friends, and even in passing with complete strangers. Whether I'm in an arena or not.

Freedom to Fully Embrace, Enjoy, and Find Quiet

What are you fighting for?

I choose to fight for, live for, and find my hope in the Creator of my fight, my life, *and* my hope.

I choose to find my joy in Christ and Christ alone. So when I am in an arena full of thousands of people singing my songs, or in a smaller, intimate venue, I still have joy. And when I walk away, into the quiet, I have joy there too. Because the Source of my joy goes before me, wherever I go.

> "Therefore everyone who hears these words of mine and puts them into practice is like a wise man who built his house on the rock. The rain came down, the streams rose, and the winds blew and beat against that house; yet it did not fall, because it had its foundation on the rock. But everyone who hears these words of mine and does not put them into practice is like a foolish man who built his house on sand. The rain came down, the streams rose, and the winds blew and beat against that house, and it fell with a great crash."
>
> When Jesus had finished saying these things, the crowds were amazed at his teaching, because he taught as one who had authority, and not as their teachers of the law.
>
> Matthew 7:24–29

If I have learned anything about life, I know that it is consistently inconsistent. We will be faced with some of the greatest times with our families, friends, and on our own, but we will also face inevitable rainstorms, streams that will rise, and winds that will blow harshly and cause damage to our dreams, hopes, health, and even our loved ones. Life is consistently inconsistent.

But one thing that remains is that when our joy is built on a firm foundation, there is no storm that can ever tear us down.

CONCLUSION

So.

If you ever find yourself awake so late that the sun starts to rise after a long day of the mundane . . .

If you ever have a moment when your mind begins to run like lightning toward a spiral of wondering if you are loved, appreciated, or understood by the people in your family or community . . .

If you ever start to doubt the choices you've made and wonder whether your tomorrow could possibly be better than yesterday . . .

If you ever feel insecure about your purpose or goals or dreams . . .

If you ever feel frustrated by a work or school schedule that feels monotonous . . .

If you ever have racing thoughts when trying to fill out applications or prepare for a presentation . . .

If you ever find yourself starting to question everything about your past, present, and even your future when faced with the absence of the noise that distracts us . . .

I challenge you to close your eyes, take a deep breath, and count to three. And for every moment following, allow yourself to embrace the silence in rhythm with your beating heart, reminding you that where there is breath there is hope, and where there is hope there is purpose. And where there is purpose there is the freedom to fully embrace, enjoy, and find quiet.

close your eyes
take a deep breath
count to three

this is finding quiet.

ACKNOWLEDGMENTS

Jesus, thank You.

While my body may be far from perfect and my mind is prone to wander, because of a hope I can only find in You, the Anchor for my soul will never be shaken. Thank You for being my constant.

Aaron, I love you. Thank you so much for both encouraging me through the process of writing this book and also taking me on random dates to distract me when writing felt like too much. Thank you for being a great man, leader, husband, and father. And to our sweet **Isabella**, I know you don't understand that I've been writing a book and why I've been busier than normal at times. But I hope that as you get older and you face things that are unknown, you will learn to trust in Christ as He brings you to find peace and quiet. And I pray that He might grant me the privilege of being a part of those moments.

Dad and Mom, thank you for the sacrifices you made to intentionally invest in yourselves, your marriage, and Morgan and me. Thank you for becoming advocates for my health, and for showing me how to love God through both triumph and tragedy.

Morgan, you are the greatest sister ever, and even though there are only two of us, I know that you would say the same. Without knowing it, you may have been the first therapist I ever had. Thank you for coaching me through the moments I was afraid I had writer's block, and for bluntly and lovingly talking me out of chapters or paragraphs that made absolutely no sense. Morgan; Patrick, my bro-in-law; and Jacob, my sweet nephew, I love all three of you.

Lydia, thank you for coming over and sitting with me when my depression was weighing so hard and I couldn't find the strength to leave the house. Kristin, thank you for being a listening ear for many anxious thoughts. Cortney and Grace, thank you for being transparent in your motherhood and walking alongside me. Melinda and Yvette, thank you for not letting me give up. Meaghan, thank you for being honest and trustworthy. Thank you to every friend I have who has ever encouraged or supported me, especially when my anxiety was through the roof and my texts were ridiculously delayed. I can't name you all, but you know who you are.

Thank you to Dr. Jorge Juncos, MD; Dr. Cheryl Tolliver, MD; Dr. Anthony Sims, DDS, IMD, DHS, PC; Dr. Jamie Marcus, MD; Catherine Miranda, NP-C, and every other doctor and medical professional who chooses to invest their wisdom and efforts in their patients and their loved ones in a way we could never repay you for. Thank you, Jessica, Meg, Joany, Kristi, Darren, and every other genuine, honest, and gracious therapist across the world.

To Patnacia Goodman and everyone at Bethany House and Baker Publishing Group, thank you for trusting me with sharing my heart and thoughts on this topic and for opening up the door for vulnerability. Thank you, Sharon Hodge, for being an editor who challenges my writing and is also a true encourager.

And last, to the woman whose name I do not know: When you told me you had a word for me, I was apprehensive. If I don't know who you are and who gave you the word, ha, I don't know if and how I should receive it. But you spoke encouragement and wisdom into my life, assuring me that I would not only write this book, but that it was precisely what God had called me to do. Without knowing my name, my story, or anything about my career, the details you spoke with grace and courage blessed me beyond measure. And I pray these words can bless others too.

Jamie Grace is a singer, songwriter, and actress. Originally from Lithonia, a small town just east of Atlanta, the two-time Grammy nominee and Dove Award-winning artist got her start on YouTube when she was only fourteen years old, creating characters for original improv sketches and sharing acoustic covers of pop, country, and CCM/Gospel songs.

With nearly 1.5 million followers across social media, Jamie Grace actively advocates for joy, wellness, and mental health through the lens of music, film, and faith. Diagnosed with Tourette Syndrome (and OCD, ADHD, and anxiety) at a young age, her resilience gives her the fuel to create content regularly, including the recent release of her devotional *Wait It Out*, as well as weekly videos and episodes of *The Jamie Grace Podcast*, in an effort to encourage others.

With four No. 1 radio singles and a gold record before she was twenty-five years old, Jamie Grace's music, videos, and podcast episodes continue to inspire everyone who listens. She is passionate about encouraging the next generation to find their voice and pursue creative avenues to share it. In 2020, Jamie Grace is releasing new music under the name Harper Still, a duo she formed with her sister, Morgan Harper Nichols.

Jamie Grace (Harper Collins) is twenty-eight and lives in Southern California with her husband, Aaron Collins, and their daughter, Isabella.